Passing the Guard

Brazilian Jiu-Jitsu Details and Techniques: volume 1

Passing the Guard

Brazilian Jiu-Jitsu Details and Techniques: volume 1

Ed Beneville

&

Tim Cartmell

GRAPPLING ARTS PUBLICATIONS, LLC
COSTA MESA, CALIFORNIA

WARNING:
Practice of the material in this book is inherently dangerous and could cause injury or death. Martial arts should be practiced under the guidance of a qualified instructor. Be mindful to avoid injuring yourself or others while practicing the material in this book. The authors and Grappling Arts Publications, LLC, deny any liability for the use or misuse of the material herein. Consult a physician before engaging in the activities demonstrated in this book. Train smart.

CREDITS

Modeling by Tim Cartmell, Pat Tasson, Matt Hwang, and Ed Beneville
Photography by Ed Beneville and Shane Lindsay.
Edited by Ed Beneville and Valerie Worthington

Copyright © 2009 by
Grappling Arts Publications, LLC.

Contact Grappling Arts Publications at info@grapplingarts.net. All rights reserved. No part of this book, including cover design and icons, may be reproduced or transmitted in any form, by any means (electronic, photocopying, recording, or otherwise), without the written permission of the authors.

International Standard Book Number: 978-0-9721097-6-5

SECOND EDITION, 2009

Printed in Korea

ABOUT THIS BOOK

We wrote this book with the assumption that intensity typically prevails over extensity. Rather than trying to touch upon all that is Brazilian jiu-jitsu, we have focused on one area - passing the guard - and tried to cover it well. We also attempt to address various situations, opportunities, and dangers that occur in the process of passing guard.

We hope this book will serve as a valuable resource to jiu-jitsu, judo, and sambo players, as well as grapplers and martial artists in general. The rules and strategies discussed throughout the book were written with Brazilian jiu-jitsu sport competition in mind. Their application, however, is much broader.

The level of material ranges from rudimentary to advanced. We make little attempt to differentiate on the basis of difficulty. What is hard for one comes easily to another. We have tried to cover the fundamentals, but that is no easy task. To a large extent, martial arts can only be learned by doing. This applies to fundamental and advanced technique alike. This book is not a substitute for training, nor for the feedback of someone who knows what he is talking about. No book or video is. On the other hand, this is a source of information, some of which is not widely taught or easily available.

It is our experience that if you are taught the same technique by three different instructors, each is likely to teach details that the others did not. To the extent that this book covers techniques with which you are already acquainted, we hope this will be the case for you.

It would have been cumbersome to both the reader and the authors to cover everything that is important every time it is important. It is the nature of grappling that the principles and details that make one technique work have applications to other techniques. Learning to improvise the details and principles learned from one technique in other situations is vital to proficiency in the art, not to mention a big part of what makes it interesting. Grappling arts require both mental and physical acumen. This book provides ideas that have applications beyond what is shown. Experiment with them, modify them, and make them your own.

All of the techniques in this book work. But none of them work when poorly executed. The difference between the success and failure of a technique sometimes comes down to a single detail. Do not give up on a technique because it is not immediately successful. It may be that you have forgotten something, your timing is off, or your opponent is a step ahead of you. First and foremost, check your positioning. Secondly, consider your training partner's reactions and resistance. For instance, if you are attempting a sweep designed to work when the opponent is driving forward, it is not going to work if he is leaning back. Good training partners are key to progressing.

Different physical attributes favor different techniques. Every player must make adjustments for his own attributes, as well as those of his opponent. Keep this in mind as you attempt to apply techniques.

We have tried to make the demonstration of technique primarily visual. To that end, the book is picture-intensive. The lion's share of the material is shown from multiple camera angles. This is necessary to clearly demonstrate all the details of a technique from start to finish and to provide perspective. The symbols and lines connecting the pictures are designed to make it easy for the eyes to follow the progression of the techniques. If you are new to this series of books, take a minute to review the Legend for an explanation of how our symbol and path system works. Alternate camera angles appear one on top of the other or side by side. Do not get hung up on slight differences in the position of the subjects from one camera angle to another. Sometimes there are differences because the photos are a little out of sync, and sometimes it has to do with variations in the reactions of the players to each other. Also, sometimes one sequence is a variation of the other, in which case the differences are described in the text.

Many of the photos are illustrated. The illustrations are meant to highlight details and, in the case of the arrows, indicate the direction(s) of the players' movements. Sometimes the highlighted items are discussed as part of the accompanying text and sometimes not, but they are always significant. In the pictures new to this second edition, the players are always interacting within a white rectangular box on the mat. The box is there to give you a better sense of the movements, angles, and distances involved in the execution of the techniques. Pay close attention to how the players move relative to the box.

This book is crammed full of photographs, and most of those photographs are accompanied by text. Sometimes the text explains things that are not apparent from the pictures, and sometimes the text describes that which is already apparent. So then, we recommend reading the text to promote your understanding of the techniques. That being said, this series of books was created with visual learners in mind. For many, this book will be first and foremost a picture book. Most readers and perusers will understand some of what is going on in the photos, but not all. We would encourage them to read the text at least where they have any questions. There are introductions to most of the techniques. The introductions place the techniques in context and sometimes include thoughts on strategy and execution. We encourage everyone to look them over.

Typically, martial arts books (and "how-to" books generally) rely on numbered pictures with corresponding numbered text. The result is that it takes some effort for the reader to figure out the sequence of the pictures and the corresponding text. We have attempted to alleviate this difficulty with a non-numeric system. The order of the pictures for a technique is delineated by lines and symbols to make recognizing their flow intuitive and obvious.

The names given to the techniques in this book are a mixture of convention and imagination. English, Portuguese, and Japanese terms are used. If you are unfamiliar with some of our terminology, it may be because we made it up.

It is our sincere hope that the material in this volume helps you expand your understanding of this dynamic art. You, the reader, are going to go through this book at your own pace. We suggest that you do not try to "finish" the book too quickly. Unless you are already an advanced practitioner, there is too much to absorb to get through it in a short period of time. Learning grappling requires a lot of doing. You probably are not going to be able to retain more than a few new techniques in your mind without committing them to muscle memory. You need to perform techniques to burn neurological pathways into your brain. When you do burn those paths, you want to do so correctly. That takes time and repetitions. That being said, it is not necessary or possible to be really good at every technique. Yet there is still value to being familiar with techniques you don't use. By being familiar with them, you will be better equipped to counter them. So then, go through this manual at whatever pace suits you, but keep in mind that there is only so much that you can absorb and make functional in one sitting.

Some techniques will work better for some players than others. This is due to a variety of factors, including skill, strength, flexibility, body type, and disposition. Keep this in mind, but do not be too quick to dismiss a technique as "not for me." All of the techniques work.

If you can learn a little more each time you get on the mat, over time you will know a lot, regardless of your level of natural ability. We hope this material will help you get there a little more quickly.

Train hard, train smart, and remember that more than anything else, success in this art requires **persistence**.

FOREWORD

I have studied jiu-jitsu under Joe Moreira (eigth degree black belt) for the past thirteen plus years. A great deal of what is contained in this book is knowledge passed to me by him. Joe's depth of martial arts know-how continues to amaze me. Some say that by the time you reach purple belt you have already seen most of what there is to know and that higher rank is mostly a matter of experience and refinement. My experience has been that there is always more to know, a fact that Joe has demonstrated through his instruction time and time again.

My interest in jiu-jitsu began when I watched Royce Gracie compete in the second installment of the Ultimate Fighting Championships. I was awed at his ability to use technique to defeat fighters who appeared physically superior. Watching him, the efficacy of the art was immediately apparent. I haven not studied directly under members of the Gracie family, but I do tip my hat to them. Their enormous contributions to the art cannot be denied; without the Gracies, there would be no Brazilian Jiu-Jitsu.

My first exposure to the sportive aspect of Brazilian jiu-jitsu was as a spectator at one of Joe Moreira's international tournaments. I went there with my friend Anthony Peters. I did not imagine at the time that I would some day be one of the competitors, much less that I would I would enjoy success as a competitor. Thanks, Tony.

My first experience in a jiu-jitsu class was with Cleber Luciano at the now defunct Brazilian Martial Arts Academy of Huntington Beach. I picked up a flyer at a bagel shop and saw that the location was convenient. I was hooked after the first class. Though Cleber was just learning English at the time, he instilled part of his own love for the art to me. For that, I am indebted to him.

Over the years, I have been fortunate to learn from many good teachers. I've found that just about everyone who has practiced for years has something valuable they can teach you. All contributed to some degree to what I know about jiu-jitsu and the content of this book.

No doubt there will be those who question who I am to make a book such as this. I make no claim to knowing more than any of those who have taught me martial arts. I produced this book because I believe that you should follow your bliss, and I love jiu-jitsu. I produced this book because I wanted to try something completely different (this time desktop publishing) as is my practice every five years or so. I produced this book because I did not believe that anyone else was about to. Since this project began, other books on Brazilian jiu-jitsu have hit the market. Still, they are different sorts of books from this one.*

*Note that the original version of this book, was written in 2001 and released in 2002. Since then the market has been flooded with BJJ books, some of which have some striking similarities to this series…I am flattered.

All the best,
Ed Beneville

ABOUT THE AUTHORS

Tim Cartmell began his martial arts training with the Chinese styles in 1972. Tim trained to the level of eighth-degree black belt in Kung Fu San Soo, and then moved to the Republic of China where he lived and studied martial arts full time for 11 years. Tim is an Asian Full-Contact fighting champion, a Submission Grappling champion, a two-time Pan American Brazilian jiu-jitsu champion at the brown and black belt level, and seven-time winner of the Copa Pacifica de Jiu-Jitsu. He received his black belt in Brazilian jiu-jitsu in 2003. Tim runs the Shen Wu Academy of Mixed Martial Arts in Garden Grove California. www.shenwu.com

Ed Beneville is a second-degree black belt under Joe Moreira and has been studying BJJ since 1996. Ed is the producer and coauthor of three books in this series: *Passing the Guard, The Guard,* and *Strategic Guard*. Ed is an experienced and accomplished competitor. He is a business and contract litigation attorney in Southern California.

ACKNOWLEDGMENTS

Ed Beneville:
Thanks to Pat Tasson for the excellent modeling work and for being a friend and training partner over the years. Thanks to James Boran, head instructor of Boran Brazilian Jiu-Jitsu, which is a great place to learn and train. The new photos in this book were taken at Boran's. Thanks to all my regular training partners: John Bennis, Pat Tasson, James Boran, Dr. Kamyar Safdari, Bill Messick, Jim Dunk, and last but certainly not least, Joe Moreira. Thanks to my wife Annette and son Connor for their love and support. Thanks to my brother Casey for helping me with so many things necessary for running Grappling Arts Publications and for being a great brother generally. Thanks to Valerie "Valhalla" Worthington (2009 brown/black *Mundial* silver medalist) for her help editing yet another one of my productions. Thanks to Howard Liu and Howard Combat Kimonos—the best.

Tim Cartmell:
I'd like to thank my teacher Cleber Luciano for his instruction. I am very proud to be Cleber's first black belt. I'd also like to thank Joe Moreira for his teachings in my early days of training, and all my teammates, students and friends for their help and support.

Contact us at: info@grapplingarts.net

(Promotional material from the original edition: Tim Cartmell is Blue, Ed Beneville is White.)

❖ LEGEND ❖

Follow the lines connecting the pictures. Symbols indicate the beginning, end, and continuations of techniques. Most techniques are shown from two or more angles. The first point of view is connected with a red line, the second with blue, and so on.

Colored backgrounds indicate a different technique on the same spread, variations, continuations, or side bars.

 go - technique starts

 go - technique starts - alternate view

 stop - end of the technique

 path turns - (down and to left)

 path turns - (from up and to right)

 path - connects the photo sequence

 path - connects alternate view

 double path - two paths merged into one

 path splits - one path becomes two

 paths merge - two paths become one

Example:
The symbols and lines indicate the order/route of the picture sequence. The numbers on this page are to clarify the progression. Photos 1-3 are the same for the red path and the blue. 4a-6a are rest of the red path, 4b-6b are the blue path; they show the same move from an alternate angle.

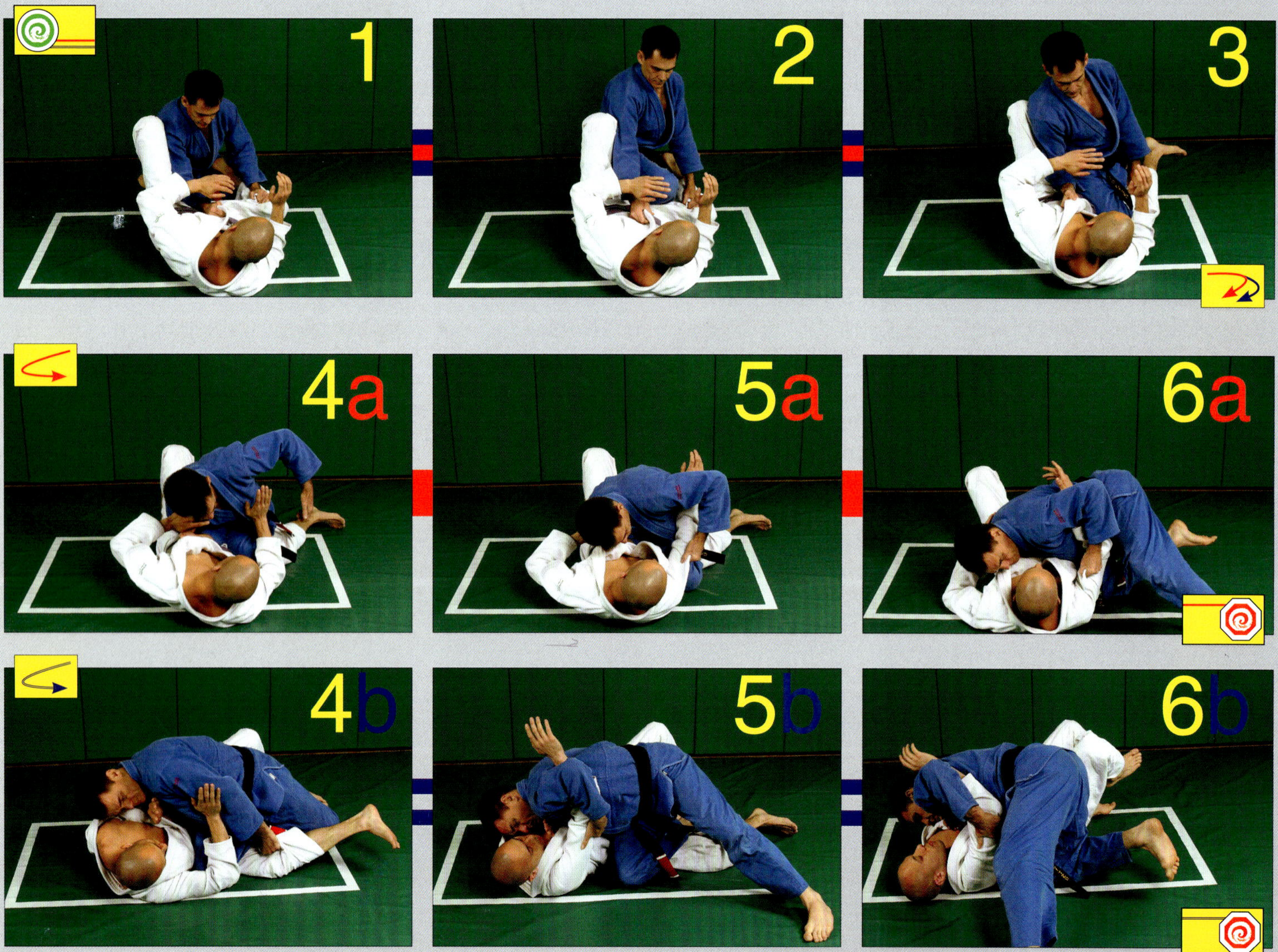

Contents

#	Chapter	Page
1	Basics	1
2	Passing from the Knees	27
3	Standing Passes	103
4	Defenses and Counters	155
5	Half Guard	203
6	Attacks	233
7	Turtle	249
8	Drills	293

Chapter 1

On Passing the Guard…

Anyone who has been exposed to Brazilian jiu-jitsu immediately becomes aware of the importance of the guard position. Fighting in the guard position will occur in almost all jiu-jitsu matches. Very often, the match will be decided by one's ability to pass the guard. Since there are more attacks from the guard position than any other position on the ground, it is vital that the fighter in the guard become proficient at passing. When fighting a skilled fighter, especially one who has a good guard, passing the guard can become very difficult. It is important to have at least several methods of passing, and to be able to flow from one technique to an other as smoothly as possible.

A number of variables must be considered when passing the guard. When inside an opponent's closed guard, you have very few options for attack. So, the first skill is to be able to break an opponent's feet open. Once the opponent's feet are open, the opportunity either to pass the guard or attack the legs is created. At all times, you must be on guard against the opponent's attack as you attempt to pass. In addition, you need to be able to pass the guard when caught in submission positions. You must be ready for sweeps and reversals that put you on your back with the opponent on top, or your opponent on your back. As you come close to passing, you need to maintain control and keep the opponent from escaping or back rolling to the knees to avoid being passed. You also have the option of attacking the opponent's legs with a variety of submission techniques: foot locks, toe holds, knee bars, etc....

There are two factors that are primary for success in passing the guard. The first is balance, or base. At all times, you must maintain a strong and balanced position. This usually requires constant adjustment on your part, depending both on what you are trying to do and what the opponent is doing. This brings up the second primary factor: sensitivity. Your opponent will be doing everything he can to stop you from passing the guard while at the same time setting up his own offensive techniques. It is extremely important to pay constant attention to the opponent's position, movement, grips, and the amount and direction of pressure he applies. When you can constantly adjust to your opponent's movement and technique and use it to set up your own techniques, you will be able to pass the guard smoothly and quickly.

There are several basic strategies for passing the guard. Variables such as size, strength, flexibility, and endurance can be brought into play depending on the type of opponent you are fighting. By becoming proficient at a number of different strategies and techniques, you can use your relative strengths to your advantage. For example, if you are larger and heavier than your opponent, you can use your weight to smash the opponent and pass. If you are smaller and lighter than your opponent, you can use your speed to pass. It is important to master several different strategies and techniques so that you are prepared for the variety of opponents you are likely to face. Even within the same weight class, you will most likely meet opponents who are considerably stronger or weaker than you, who are more or less flexible than you, etc. You need to be flexible in your game to adjust to different kinds of fighters. Finally, in competitive matches, the score and time remaining will also influence your strategy and the types of technique used.

Conclusion: Whether or not you ever become proficient at a wide variety of passes, you should be aware of many strategies and techniques. By doing so you will be better equipped to attack and defend the myriad variables and situations you will sooner or later face.

Posture and Base

Above all else, your posture and base (balance) will determine your success in passing the guard. Without base, your opponent will have little trouble applying a submission or a sweep. Without base, you will not have the power to open your opponent's feet and control him as you pass. The correct alignment of your torso and limbs and the ability to adjust your position constantly to maintain balance are key to successful guard passing. In order to maintain balance and a strong position, you will need to be relaxed. Relaxation will allow you to move freely and quickly while simultaneously remaining sensitive to your opponent's movements and attacks.

The most important factor in determining whether or not your structure is strong and balanced is the placement of your head. Since your head is at the top of your spine, the placement and movement of the head directly influences the entire balance of your body. In general, you want to stretch your spine to its full length and lift up from the crown of your head, keeping your chin slightly tucked in when beginning a pass from the guard. Once you collapse your chest and slump forward, you will lose the ability to generate force, and it will be easier for the opponent to control and move you. When in the guard, a slumped-over posture makes it especially easy for your opponent to pull your head down for a choke or to set up an armbar or triangle choke.

When passing from your knees in the opponent's guard, before you start your pass you should begin sitting on your heels with a fairly wide base, knees spread apart. The wider the base, the greater the stability. Your head should be up with the back straight, your hands on the opponent in an appropriate grip position. Your body should resemble the shape of a pyramid, with the head positioned at about the mid-point between your hands and feet.

Grips need to be taken carefully in order to guard against loss of balance and prevent submissions. Extending the arm too far up the opponent's body in the wrong positions, or holding with the elbows opened out to the sides, can leave you vulnerable to wrist, elbow, and shoulder submissions. In general, the elbows should be closed inward and kept down and 'heavy.' The wrists should not be bent too far upward or downward. The hands should grip the opponent's body and limbs, and should rarely be placed on the mat. Remember: The position of the grip will determine not only the options available to pass, but also your overall stability. The position of your arms should always act to strengthen your base, your arm often acting as a "third leg." This becomes especially important when changing the position of your base or when stepping with the feet.

Let's discuss the center of gravity. We all know that the lower the center of gravity and the wider the base, the more stable the object. Obviously, since

An example of the use of base: The player on the bottom tries to sweep Ed by elevating one of his legs and pushing on the other. Ed posts his left leg out which helps him to keep from getting turned over. Ed

INTRODUCTION

our goal is not to sit motionless in the guard but to pass it or counter-attack, we need to find the dynamic balance between stability and mobility. Generally, we need to keep our center of gravity as low as possible, even as we move. This is usually accomplished by keeping the hips lower than the head. There are exceptions, of course. These less commonly seen techniques involve "jumping" over the guard with the hips rising high. These techniques are inherently unstable and must be used with correct timing and position.

Besides keeping the weight low, many guard pass techniques will involve forward pressure and "smashing" the opponent with your weight. Since you are either on your knees or standing when you pass, you have the advantage of gravity on

the opponent for control, or to help you maneuver quickly around the opponent.

Maintaining your balance while in movement is vital. As you pass the guard, you can use your feet, knees, hips, shoulders, elbows, or head to post on the ground or your opponent to make base. Standing up without an appropriate grip leaves you vulnerable to sweeps. You should typically have at least one hand gripping or posting on the opponent at all times as you pass the guard. Think of a table; it is most stable with its four legs in place. If one leg is broken off, the table may still stand, but it will not be as stable. A table balanced on two legs is extremely unstable, and a small amount of force will cause it to tip over and fall. Not only your hands and feet, but also your knees, hips, shoulders, elbows and head,

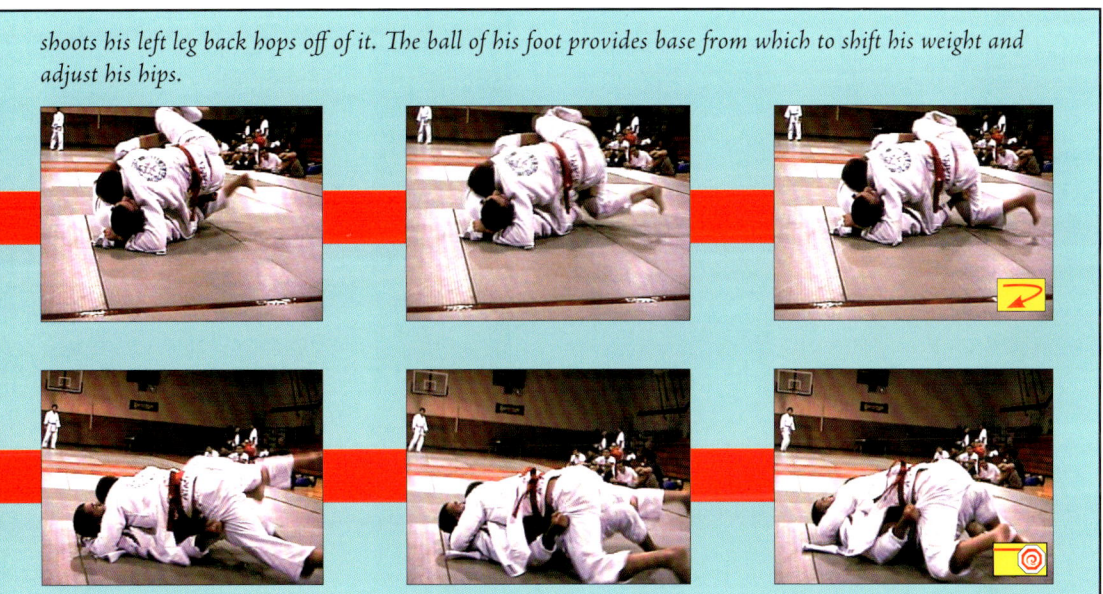

shoots his left leg back hops off of it. The ball of his foot provides base from which to shift his weight and adjust his hips.

can be used to post on the opponent or the mat. Try to have at least three if not four points stabilizing your base as you position yourself and pass the guard.

One final point: When you are attempting to pass the guard and the opponent begins to compromise your base or you feel your balance is threatened, consider coming back to a stable base position to prevent a sweep or submission

your side. By remaining relaxed, with the center of gravity low and pressing into the opponent, you can conserve energy while forcing your opponent to work hard in order to maintain his position. In addition, your upright position when passing allows you to use not only the weight of your center against the opponent, but also the power of your legs. It will be difficult to control an opponent's hips and legs with the strength of your arms alone. But with correct posture and stable center of gravity, you will be able to use the power of your legs to press your weight into

before resuming the guard pass.

4 FUNDAMENTALS ❖ TYPES OF GUARD

What is the Guard?

There are three main types of guard: closed, open, and half. In closed guard your opponent has his legs wrapped around your torso and his ankles crossed. Most, but not all, attacks from the closed guard require your opponent to "open" his guard—uncross his ankles—at some point. In half guard, one of your legs is to the outside of your opponent's legs, but your other leg is between his legs. Open guard is a broader term than closed guard or half guard and consists of all the other guard positions. All guards have one thing in common: Your opponent's legs are in the way of your obtaining a dominant position like the mount, side control, or the back. You need to pass the guard for most submissions. There are some submissions that work from within the guard (see **Ch. 6**), but unless your opponent senses some threat that you will pass, they are hard to get. So then you must be proficient at passing the guard.

Closed guard: The guard player's ankles are crossed, *closed* around his opponent's torso.

Open guard: The guard player's feet are open. Open guard allows the guard player more freedom of movement and opportunities to use his legs to attack. **There are many open guard variations.**

Half-guard: One of the guard passer's legs is outside his opponent's legs; the other is trapped.

Sitting guard: Instead of playing on his back, the guard player sits up. Typically, the guard player hooks his feet behind your legs and tries to hug around your back.

Spider guard involves the guard player pulling one or both of your sleeve ends while pushing into one or both of your biceps with the feet.

X-guard: The guard player's insteps hook around both sides of your leg, the crossed shins making an X.

De la Riva: One of the guard player's legs threads behind one of the passer's legs, then hooks in front of the other.

Butterfly guard: The guard player's insteps hook your legs from the inside. The guard player can play from a seated position or on his back.

POSTURE

POSTURE

Posture is vital to passing the guard. Without good posture, the risk of being swept or submitted increases dramatically. Your opponent should continually try to undermine your posture, and you should continually make adjustments to fix it. We begin here with a basic posture for fighting out of the guard from your knees.

When sitting in your opponent's guard, keep your back straight, your rear sitting over your feet, and your hands appropriately gripping on the opponent's body. Although the hand and leg placement will vary according to the situation and technique applied, some fundamental alignments should be maintained. First, the overall alignment of the body is 'pyramid' shaped. Viewed from the side, the head should be near the midpoint between the hands and the feet. Leaning too far forward or backward compromises the base and makes it difficult either to control the opponent's movement or defend against his attacks.

Blue demonstrates basic posture from the knees within the guard. This posture is a starting point. You will need to move out of it as you pass the guard. Though your posture will necessarily have to change as you pass the guard, you must be mindful to maintain good base as you go. The purpose of good posture is twofold: It provides good base, and it affords you protection from submission attempts.

Wide-apart knees give you stable base.

Your butt is low, your head is up, and your back is straight.

Keep one or both hands in front of your head.

Here, we see Blue sitting in guard with good posture. With a grip under White's armpits, Blue is holding the gi and keeping his elbows in, making it difficult for White to attack his arm, sit up to attack the neck, or sweep. At this point, Blue keeps his knees to the outside of White's hips and his back straight. His hands are out in front of his head. Blue places his hands in White's armpits with the four fingers inside the armpits and the thumb hooked over the top of White's shoulders.

Staggering the hands provides extra stability.

Keeping the head up protects the neck.

Blue staggers his hands. He makes his hands into fists, holding White's gi and making sure to keep his head behind an imaginary vertical plane rising from his lead (left) hand. This helps keep White from breaking Blue's base forward, which he will try to do by pulling on Blue's neck or lapels.

FUNDAMENTALS ❖ BASE & ALIGNMENT

CAGING THE HIPS

Keep your knees wide apart. Keep your opponent centered in front of you.

Use the insides of your legs to block his hips.

If you establish good posture, your opponent will need to do something to disrupt your base to open up attacks for him. Most of his options require him to move his hips one way or another. By following his hips with your own, you can stop many of his techniques before they start. The wide base you want with your knees not only provides you with stability, it also allows you to use the insides of your legs to block your opponent's hip movements. Keep your lower spine lined up with his. First, use the inside of your leg to block his hip, then change the position of your knees as necessary to keep them centered. Keep your butt down and your hips low as you do. You may have to lift your hips in order to move, but keep it to a minimum.

White attacks with an armbar from the guard. In order to make the attack work, his hips have to move out to one side. Blue gets into a bad spot because he fails to adjust as White attacks.

White attempts the same armbar as above. This time, however, Blue immediately cages White's hips, nullifying the armbar.

If he moves, you move.

Keep your opponent's spine in line with your own for defense.

White and Blue's spines are lined up. This is good for Blue, bad for White.

White shifts his hips out for the armbar. Blue lifts his hips. Although this sacrifices his posture momentarily, it also allows him to better reposition his own hips by moving his knee.

Blue moves his right knee forward and puts White's hips back between the insides of his upper legs, killing White's attack.

BASE & ALIGNMENT

Here is another example of not caging the hips and getting attacked, and then of preventing the attack by caging the hips.

White moves his hips away from Blue's center-line, pushes Blue's chest with his right hand, and moves his right knee under Blue's left armpit and in front of Blue's chest. White ends in a better position for him to attack and a more difficult position for Blue to pass.

White begins the same move as above.

Blue traps White's right thigh by pinching it between his arm and his side. Blue's left elbow moves toward the top of his own left thigh and his head moves that way also.

Blue's left knee pushes into Whites right buttock. White's right upper leg is controlled by a triangle consisting of Blue's left side, arm and thigh.

Blue moves his left knee forward and to White's outside. Blue's objective is to keep White centered and to control White's ability to move his hips.

Blue centers himself to White.

Of course, Blue needs to do more than just shut down White's attacks; he needs to go on the offensive himself. But by shutting White down, Blue gives himself the chance to dictate how he will pass the guard instead of trying to fight his way out of White's game. Now that the situation is neutral, Blue will take the initiative and force White to catch up to him.

8 FUNDAMENTALS ❖ HAND POSITIONING

STAGGERING HANDS

In order to keep yourself from getting pulled down, stagger your hands. This provides for good base while simultaneously allowing you to work one arm back to help with opening the legs.

Elbows in, thumbs up.

ELBOWS IN, THUMBS UP

Elbows in and thumbs up is good positioning for the arms when you are opening the guard. By dropping your weight onto your elbows, you can make pressure both to control your opponent's hips and break open his legs. Positioning the thumbs up allows you to use your grips as anchors or leverage points for pushing the elbows down. Here, Blue's left elbow is to the inside of White's right leg. Positioning it there hides it from White and protects Blue from triangle and armbar attacks. You need to be careful to protect your elbows (next spread).

GRIPPING

Here we see a correct way to grip in the guard. Blue has his hands staggered, the left hand holding the lapel at the lower chest and the right hand holding at the hip. This grip allows Blue to control White's movement. Blue limits White's ability to attack while maintaining his own base in preparation for breaking the guard. Notice how Blue keeps his elbows locked in tightly. Note also that he is gripping the gi pants.

Keep your knees wide and your butt down.

⊙ It is helpful to be able to use your insteps for base. If you cannot, work on it. Eventually (after plenty of cramps in your arches) the flexibility will come... eventually.

There are a number of good grips for the forward hand. Here Blue takes both of White's lapels with his right hand while the left holds the gi pants.

⊙ Grabbing either lapel or the cloth works also. If Blue did not hold on at all, White could easily pull Blue's arm into a position to attack it.

Hands and Gripping

How tightly to grip.

If you grip the opponent's gi too tightly, it is easy to fatigue your hands. Sensitivity to when a tight grip is desirable saves energy. If your opponent is not fighting your grip, don't tire your fingers by over-gripping. That being said, you must stay ready to tighten your grip if the opponent tries to force his way free of it and you do not want him to. Most players give clues before they try to break free; learn to spot them. With your grips in place, it is possible to tighten your grip quickly when need be.

Sleeve grips

Where you hold the sleeves is a function of the technique you will be using. If you are holding the elbows or triceps, you will generally shape your hand as if holding a bottle. If you hold the gi instead, you almost always want most of the grip's power to come from your pinky, ring, and middle finger, like a pistol grip. Use the thumb to help gather the cloth, but not so much for the actual gripping.

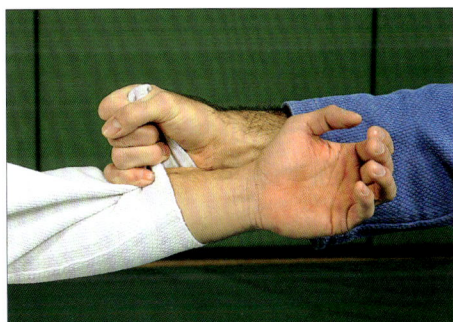

With this grip, the hand holds the cloth with all fingers outside of the material.

This method involves gripping the cloth with the four fingers wrapped inside the material, thumb on the outside.

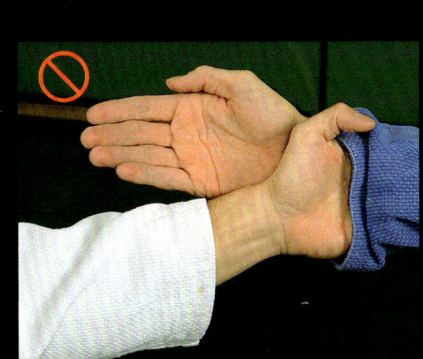

This is an illegal grip. It is against BJJ and Judo rules to grab inside the sleeves.

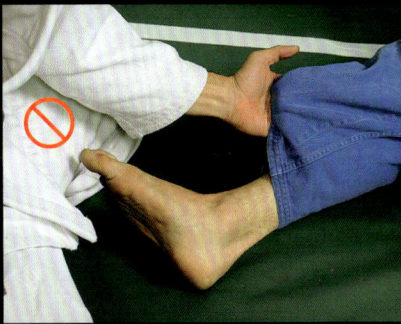

This is also an illegal grip. You cannot grab inside the cuff. One reason these grips are forbidden is because of the potential danger to the fingers if the opponent twists his arm or leg. That being said, they are effective if the opponent does not twist his limb, and sometimes even if they do.

Where to grip the legs:

This is a good way to grip the legs when passing the guard. Blue's hands are to the inside of White's knees, and he is ready to use his forearms to parry White's shins. Blue's thumbs are turned back toward himself with his palms down, and his wrists kept straight.

Blue anchors his left hand while dropping weight down onto that elbow.

You typically want to hold your opponent's legs at or above the knees when passing the guard. Use your forearms and elbow to block the movement of your opponent's upper legs. That alone is enough to stop most triangle and juji-gatame (armbar) attempts.

These are poor grips. White's thumbs are pointed up which is awkward and puts too much pressure on the wrist. Though he is correctly holding the inside of Blue's knees, White's elbows and forearms are to the outside of Blue's legs.

PREVENTATIVE GRIPPING

Once you establish good posture, you need to go on the offensive. You will need to move your arms from place to place as you pass guard. But there are many pitfalls to passing the guard. Sometimes your opponent may get control of one of your arms. If that happens, you need to consider grabbing something before you get into trouble. The opponent's gi is usually a good bet, but also use the palms of your hands against his body, as if you had no gi. On this page are two examples. Remember, if your opponent wants something, you probably should not let him have it.

Blue's base looks pretty good, but nevertheless, White manages to get both his arms behind Blue's left elbow and begins to drag it forward.

Blue does not want White dragging his arm. Blue grabs White's lapel. The lapels get used a lot as anchors, as they are sturdy and easy to grip.

As White pulls Blue's arm forward his lapel is pulled tight because of Blue's grip, and White can pull Blue no further. Blue's position has not been compromised much.

Elbow positioning blocks White's right leg, should White open his guard.

Instead of pulling Blue forward, as above, White begins by dragging Blue's arm across his body.

As above, Blue uses his hand as an anchor to stop White from dragging his arm across his body. This time, not only does Blue grab the lapel, but he also drops his elbow to White's side for added resistance and contact.

Hands and Gripping

Hands and elbows
Sometimes your opponent will get control of one of your arms as you try to pass his guard. Usually he goes for your elbow or your wrist. If he goes for your wrist, drop that elbow. If he goes for your elbow, grab something with that hand. In other words, if he attacks one, defend with the other.

White is starting to get control of Blue's right elbow. That could quickly become a problem for Blue.

Blue defends his elbow by dropping his weight onto it while gripping White's gi, thumb up, with his right hand. Blue keeps his elbow tight against White's left leg, controlling White's hips by trapping White's upper leg.

Attack

White's right hand grabs Blue's right sleeve and he connects his hands in a figure-four grip.

White breaks the grip and proceeds to drag Blue's arm across his body. This is bad for Blue; his back is exposed and he is vulnerable to submissions.

Defense

Once again, White tries to use a figure-four grip to break Blue's grip and attack.

The simple solution to White's figure-four grip is, once again, for Blue to drop his elbow. Even if White strips Blue's grip, Blue's elbow is dug in, and his arm is not going anywhere.

12 FUNDAMENTALS ❖ HANDS AND GRIPPING

ARM DRAGS

The easiest way to prevent your opponent from dragging your arm across his body is to grab something; your gi, his gi, or your other arm.

> More arm drag counters at pages 196-197, Ch. 4: **Defenses**.

White grabs Blue's wrist and elbow in preparation for the arm drag.

White pulls Blue's right arm across to his right side.

Continuing, White sits up and hugs around Blue's back with his left arm. White is now in a good position to attack.

White prepares to arm drag Blue's right arm.

Blue immediately grabs White's right lapel with his left hand.

Blue pushes away with his left arm and leans toward his own right side to prevent White from dragging his.

GRIP COUNTERS

You can save yourself a lot of work if you prevent potentially dangerous lapel grips right away.

> More collar grip counters at pages 159-162, Ch. 4: **Defenses**.

White grabs Blue's lapel with his right hand.

Blue grabs around the outsides of White's wrist with both hands, wrapping the thumbs under the bottom of White's wrist and his four fingers over the top of the wrist.

Blue simultaneously pushes White's wrist away with his hands and leans his body back to break the grip.

POSTURE

Bad Hand Placement

Instructors often say never to put your hand on the mat while passing the guard. It is not quite as simple as that. For instance, sometimes you need to post a hand to stop a sweep. Most of the time, however, you definitely do not want to put your hands on the mat to your opponent's sides from within a standard guard like the one pictured. Here, White sits up and grabs a *Kimura*. The hip-bump sweep is also a high percentage attack against this mistake.

Do not put your hands on the mat.

> Defenses to a variety of attacks from the guard appear in Ch. 4: **Defenses**.

Fix Your Head

Good upright sitting posture goes a long way toward preventing your head from being pulled down and preventing chokes. But often you have to lower your head to pass, and other times your opponent will find a way to get hold of your head or neck. Here is a simple defense.

Don't drop your head too much (like in this photo).

White pulls the back of Blue's head.

Blue keeps his butt low and digs his palms into White's torso. Holding the belt and digging in under the bottom rib are good hand position options.

Blue pushes down and forward with his arms while letting his head drop until it is clear of White's hands, then his head moves away and up.

Posture provides stability and defense.

Blue does not want to have to fix his head again. His left hand on White's chest keeps White from sitting up.

14 FUNDAMENTALS ❖ ARM PLACEMENT

USING THE ELBOW

The single under-hook guard pass is both fundamental and effective. However, there is a fair amount of misconception about the effectiveness of the pass. It is true that if the pass is done incorrectly, you will leave yourself open to armbar and triangle attacks (next spread). However, if you correctly position your non-under-hooking elbow, it is the most effective tight passing technique. You **must** use your elbow to block the inside of the leg you are not under-hooking.

Here, Blue shows proper grip and elbow placement for an under-hook guard pass. Note Blue's left elbow is pulled back and is pressing down deep inside White's right leg.

Blue lowers his body and slides White's left leg onto his right shoulder.

Blue keeps head pressure outward against White's left leg as he pushes downward inside White's right leg with his left elbow. White is unable to pull Blue's left arm or raise his own right leg to set up the triangle.

✱ For the purposes of better illustrating the use of his left elbow, Blue is allowing White's hips considerably more space then he normally would if he were passing the guard against a resisting opponent.

Arm Placement

Bad Elbow Placement

White fails to use his left elbow to block the inside of Blue's right leg. White has poor control of Blue's hips. This puts White's left arm in danger.

Here, White is making the mistake of reaching his left arm in too high, towards Blue's head. Making matters worse he is leaving his right arm behind without doing enough to control Blue's left leg. This is a common novice mistake.

With the arm extended, it is easy for Blue to catch White in a triangle choke...

... or an armbar.

16 Fundamentals ❖ Breaking Grips

Breaking grips

Sometimes your opponent will attempt to control the ends of your gi sleeves. When they do, there are a couple basic approaches. One is to grab onto something before your arm winds up in a bad position (page 12). Another option is to free your arm using small-circle jiu-jitsu. Here Blue demonstrates how he can break White's grip by circling his trapped arm in either direction. Sometimes the first direction you attempt does not work for one reason or another. Most of the time the solution is to switch to circling the other way.

Circling out

White grabs the outside of Blue's sleeve.

Blue move moves his hand down inside White's wrist.

Continuing, Blue circles his hand up from the outside of White's wrist.

Blue twists his hand palm up and chops inward into the back of White's wrist, breaking his grip.

Circling in

White grabs the outside of Blue's sleeve.

Blue circles his hand over the top to the outside of White's wrist, turning his thumb down.

Blue continues to circle his hand up inside White's wrist. The thumb side edge of Blue's wrist grinds against the thumb side edge of White's wrist.

Leverage breaks White's grip as Blue twists his hand palm up over the top of White's wrist.

BREAKING OPEN THE CLOSED GUARD

BREAKING OPEN THE CLOSED GUARD

Now that we have an idea of how to make posture and protect our arms, it is time to break open the opponent's legs in order to pass the guard. The rest of the techniques in this chapter are concerned with breaking open the closed guard from your knees. Some of the techniques involve using the points of the elbows to cause pain to the opponent's quadriceps to open his legs. Sometimes that is not enough, and you need to put your back into it also. Sometimes putting your back into it is enough by itself, and sometimes a knee on the tailbone combines with putting your back into it. Finally, you can stack your opponent into the can opener and attack the neck. **Ch. 3** shows techniques for breaking open the closed guard from a standing position. You need to become adept at various approaches and be ready to switch from one to the other. Once the legs are open, you can stand or kneel to pass.

BACK PRESSURE

Using your torso to overpower your opponent's limbs is at the heart of a good deal of BJJ. Using your back, especially your lower back, is key to opening the closed guard. The technique on this page relies on pressure from the lower back. Blue's arms are involved, but their function is to keep White's hips down and to stop White from following him, not to push. Blue lifts his hips while pinning White's hips. Blue is using the traction his knees have to the mat as points of leverage.

Blue sets his base and controls White by gripping under his armpits. He is careful to keep his elbows in.

Blue adjusts his grips so that his right hand holds White's belt and his left hand holds the front edge of White's right hip.

⊘ Note that the head comes in front of the hands during part of this technique. There are few absolutes in Brazilian jiu-jitsu. Sometimes it is useful to pass this way. Blue is more susceptible to being pulled forward, however.

Blue begins to shoot his hips backward while pushing with his arms. Blue's lower back is putting pressure against White's calves.

Continuing the backward thrust of the hips and forward push of the arms, Blue breaks the guard by literally putting his back into it.

18 FUNDAMENTALS ❖ BREAKING OPEN THE CLOSED GUARD

KNEE-IN-BUTT

The knee-in-butt method of opening the guard combines back pressure, a strong mechanical base, and discomfort, to open the guard. It is one of the most effective methods.

Blue postures and staggers his grip.

Blue opens his left knee outward to widen his base, then slides his right knee into White's rear.

Blue want his kneecap centered on White's tailbone. Blue slides his left leg back and pushes forward with his arms as he begins to turn to his left.

Blue continues moving his lower back backward, twisting his hips and pushing forward by lowering his weight into his arms while pushing with them to break White's guard.

Blue drives White's right leg to the ground with his weight and maintains control over White's hips in preparation for the pass.

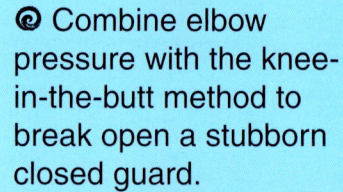

◉ Combine elbow pressure with the knee-in-the-butt method to break open a stubborn closed guard.

◀ Here, White fails to do anything to put downward pressure on Blue's hips. Blue easily counters the attempt to break open his legs by lifting his butt on top of White's thigh.

BREAKING OPEN THE CLOSED GUARD

USING ELBOWS TO OPEN THE GUARD

On this spread are techniques for making extra pressure and/or pain with the elbows to open the guard. On this page, Blue breaks open the guard by jamming the point of his elbow into White's quadriceps with his hands staggered. Blue sinks the weight of his upper body into his elbows. This technique can be used by itself or in conjunction with back pressure and knee-in-the-butt methods. It certainly is more effective if you do put your torso into it.

Blue sets his grips in preparation for the guard break.

Blue looks over his right shoulder and moves his right elbow inside White's left knee.

Blue looks back, brings his weight up over his right elbow.

Blue now drives his body weight down into his right elbow as he pushes back with his hips, forcing White's feet open. Notice Blue has placed his left knee behind White's rear.

◉ Blue's elbow presses into the sensitive area at the inside of White's lower thigh. The point of his elbow digs into the inside of White's quadriceps and the top of the knee joint. The grip of his right hand is an anchor that allows him to transmit more pressure through his elbow. Blue will drop weight into his right elbow while pushing down with his right shoulder.

Both of Blue's elbows block the insides of White's knees.

Blue moves his hips back to prevent White from closing his guard again.

20 FUNDAMENTALS ❖ BREAKING OPEN THE CLOSED GUARD

SINGLE ELBOW

Blue begins to set up his grips in preparation for breaking the guard.

Blue grips White's chest lapel with his right hand, keeping his arm straight as he grips Blue's right pants with his left hand.

Blue keeps his left elbow close to his side and presses downward into the inside of White's right knee. Blue has also extended his right arm and is beginning to push backward.

Blue slides his left knee back to stabilize his base and make space for his right knee to move into the center of White's rear.

With his right knee in the center of White's rear, Blue moves his hips back and twists to his left. The pressure of Blue's hips breaks White's feet open.

Maintaining the forward pressure with his arms, Blue prepares to pass the guard.

DOUBLE ELBOW

Blue postures up and grips White's pants. Blue brings his elbows close to his sides and inside White's knees.

Blue brings his weight over his elbows and begins to drive his elbows down as he pushes back against White's feet with his hips.

Blue continues to push down with his elbows and back with his hips and breaks White's guard.

Breaking Open the Closed Guard

Structure and Bounce

This technique is a good example of using structure. By posting the sole of his foot on the mat, Blue keeps White's leg from coming down on that side. At the same time, White's other leg has nothing under it for support. This allows Blue to use gravity and his top position to his advantage as stretches up to get his hand on White's knee, then drops his weight down onto White's unsupported leg.

Blue has set up good posture. His grips are staggered and his elbows are in.

Blue's torso twists as he moves his right knee back. Blue arms keep White's torso right where it was.

Blue lifts his right leg, placing the sole of his foot on the mat at his right side, far enough back so that White cannot grab his ankle. Blue is careful to keep his back straight and weight down.

Raising his hips straight up, Blue places his left hand on the inside of White's right knee.

Blue presses straight downward on White's leg (using a rapid bouncing motion if necessary) to begin sliding White's leg down to the mat.

White's feet break apart and Blue pins White's right leg to the mat with his left hand and then his left knee.

22 FUNDAMENTALS ❖ THE CAN OPENER

Blue grabs the back of White's head with both hands, placing the heels of his palms at the base of White's head.

> ⊙ The can opener is banned as a submission in most BJJ competitions. Sometimes, however, it is allowed if you use it as a way of opening your opponent's closed guard.

Blue pinches his elbows in close together and squeezes his wrists together against the sides of White's neck. It is very important not to leave space between your wrists and the opponent's neck.
Blue keeps his elbows close together and pressed against the front of White's chest. Blue lifts his hands while digging in with his elbows: a sort of biceps curl.

Blue pulls back with both hands, forcing White's chin against his chest as he simultaneously drives his elbows into White's chest. The pressure causes the back of White's neck to be stretched painfully. This technique may cause the opponent to submit, but is most often used as a method of breaking the opponent's guard; the opponent will be forced to open his guard and push you away to relieve the pressure on his neck.

> ⊙ Blue begins the can opener as described above, but hops up onto the balls of his feet to amplify the pressure applied to White's neck. Blue moves his feet forward and continues applying the pressure to White's neck until White's guard opens. Blue ends in a good position to pass the guard.

As he pulls on White's head, Blue commits his base forward onto his elbows, and his hips rise.

Forward momentum and a lot of weight on White's chest make Blue's lower body light, allowing him to pop up on his feet.

Blue establishes base with his feet.

Blue sits on the back of White's legs. This puts additional torque on White's neck.

White opens his legs to relieve the pressure on his neck.

> From here, consider the step-over pass on pages 122-123.

Combat base

Once you open the guard, you need to keep it open so that you can pass. One easy way to keep it open as you decide your attack is with combat base. From combat base, overlapping an elbow and its same side knee nullifies a number of attacks from the guard. The overlap creates a barrier through which your opponent's leg cannot pass, as in the examples to the right. Besides being a relatively safe position against the open guard, passing the guard with a knee up and the sole of the foot on the mat is desirable in a number of situations, including knee-through-the-middle type passes, as we will see in the next two chapters.

Blue overlaps his right elbow to the outside of his right knee. His right hand holds White's lapel for added stability.

This time, Blue overlaps his elbow to the inside. Either way is good. For some guard passes, one way will be preferable to the other, though it is easy enough to switch when need be.

Examples of things going wrong

Here are three examples of things that can go wrong when the sole of your foot is on the mat and you do not overlap the knee and elbow.

▲ White slips his left knee inside Blue's right arm. From here he can use his knee in Blue's chest and his hold on Blue's arm to move Blue's upper body.

▲ Because Blue did not overlap, White was able to put his left foot on Blue's hip, push away, and move his knee against Blue's triceps.

▲ Without the overlap, White is able to get an underhook.

Fundamentals:

◉ Posture, base, and alignment, are your first priorities while in the guard.

Posture: There is not a single definition of good posture, but generally you want your butt low, knees wide, head up, and hand in front of you.

Base: Base is related to posture. The mat, your arms, and your legs provide base. So can your head and your opponent. Use good positioning to increase the stability of your base. Here are two example of using the hands for base:

1. Hold your opponent's armpits to stop him from sitting up or pulling you down. Keep your head up.

2. One arm keeps your opponent from sitting up or getting a deep collar grip, while the other helps control their hips.

Alignment: By staying aligned with your opponent's center-line, you can nullify many attacks.

Fix your posture, if and when it is compromised, before attempting to pass, and you will avoid many pitfalls.

◉ How you place your hands and elbows is important for both offense and defense.

Stagger your hands for stability and to allow you to twist your torso.

Grip inside the knees to control your opponent's knees as you pass.

Anchors: Grab what you can to anchor down your arms and keep them safe. Keep your elbows down and in.

Grip fighting: By preventing dangerous grips, you avoid the attacks that come with them.

Elbow placement is vital for controlling the inside of one of you opponent's legs when you lift under the other. Proper use of your elbow will nullify triangle and armbar attacks.

Circle your hand in or out to break open pesky sleeve grips.

 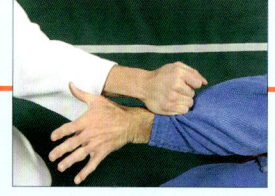  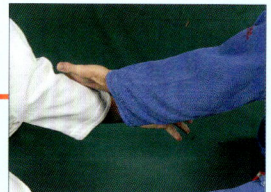

Opening closed guard:

Back pressure: Brace against your opponent's hips with your arms as you use gravity and the strength or your lower back to push into their heels. This type of back pressure is used to many guard openers.

Knee-in-butt: Your kneecap blocks your opponent's tailbone. This prevents him from following you as you use back pressure to open the legs.

Elbows: Use your elbows to block your opponent's legs and to make him uncomfortable. Drop weight into him and use back pressure to compound the pressure.

Single elbow: Use the rear elbow against the inside of your opponent's quadriceps. As you back out, use your elbow as base and concentrate your weight on it.

Double elbow: Keep your shoulders square and rise slightly. Your elbows go inside his, quads and you drop your weight into them as you spread them open.

Twisting pressure: Brace your opponent's hips with your arms. Post a foot out slightly, then lift that knee. Lifting the knee creates space and back pressure to open the guard.

Bouncing pressure: If twisting does not open the guard, finish the job by bracing your palm on the inside of his knee and bouncing weight into it.

Can opener: By cranking your opponent's neck, you force him to open his legs or tap.

Standing can opener: You can increase your leverage and range of motion by standing as you apply the can opener.

Combat base: Once you open the guard, overlap your elbow and kneecap when your knee is in the middle of your opponent's legs. Your other hand controls the inside of his knee. This is a good position for passing the guard.

knee inside elbow

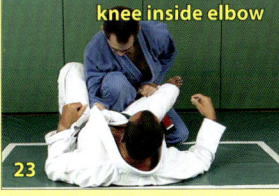

elbow inside knee

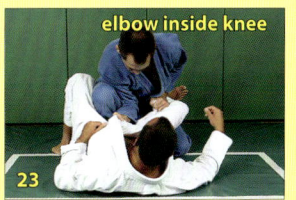

grapplingarts.net

Chapter 2

Overview

There are many ways to pass the guard and many possible submission opportunities once the opponent's feet are open. There are two basic positions from which the guard is passed: standing and from the knees. Kneeling passes allow you to keep your center of gravity low and your base wide. Standing passes allow you to put more downward crushing pressure on the opponent, and mobility is greater.

There are three basic methods for passing the guard: under the legs, over the legs, or around the legs. Techniques can and should be used in combination. Once the opponent's feet are open, opportunities for leg submissions present themselves. During the pass, there is opportunity to set up foot locks, knee bars, toe holds, key locks, and heel hooks.

It is important to be proficient at several different ways to pass the guard. It is unlikely you will be able to pass the guard of a skilled opponent with the first pass attempted. Very often, especially with a strong opponent, your best chance of passing is to flow with his technique and take the opportunity given. A flexible strategy is usually best, unless you can dominate an opponent with strength or weight. Another strategy that can be employed, especially as a last resort, is to bait the opponent with an opportunity for submission and then pass as he attacks. For example, you extend your arm up high, wait for the opponent to attack with an armbar, and then defend the armbar, giving you an opportunity to pass. This is a delicate game; the threat of submission is close. Although less commonly seen, passes that involve jumping or rolling over the opponent have a surprise element and sometimes provide the best means to pass. It is good to be familiar with jumping and rolling passes.

When you are larger and stronger than your opponent, passes that are based on crushing or smashing the opponent are often best applied. These types of passes require constant forward pressure and weight. When facing a larger or stronger opponent, passes involving speed may be a better choice.

This chapter will focus on passes from the knees. We begin with the most basic of the passes. It is also one of the most reliable and effective, with or without the gi.

Do not mistake basic moves for ones that will not work against a skilled opponent. Sometimes basic is best. Of course, if you are limited to one or two passes and your opponent knows them, that can be a problem. Also keep in mind that even simple moves sometimes have many fine points, any one of which can mean the difference between success and failure.

Passing the Guard from the Knees

The most basic guard passes are from the knees. Most beginners will learn to open the guard while on the knees and then pass the guard while keeping one knee on the mat. Breaking and passing the guard from the knees is more stable than standing to pass; the center of gravity is lower and the base wider. Although you can of course be swept from the knees, because of the lower center of gravity you will usually be more successful at stopping sweep attempts. On the other hand, the risk of getting caught in an armbar, choke, or triangle is somewhat higher when passing from the knees. Another downside to the increased stability of low guard passes is the decrease in potential speed. Just as we can obviously run faster on our feet than on our knees, you will not have the same speed and ability for rapid changes in direction that you would have standing.

One advantage of passing from the knees is conservation of energy. In general, it requires less energy to pass from the knees than from the feet. This will become an important factor in matches where you are already fatigued but need to pass the guard (when you are down on points, for example). In addition, most low passes involve staying very close and tight to the opponent's hips. Controlling the opponent's hips greatly restricts his freedom of motion, while at the same time allowing you to use gravity and your weight to your advantage. You can conserve your own energy while constantly forcing the opponent to work against your weight. If you are stronger and heavier than your opponent, these types of passes may be most effective for you.

Passing close to the opponent on the knees also limits the variations of the guard available to the opponent. For example, passing close and low prevents the opponent from using the spider guard (feet on your biceps) or De la Riva guard (leg threaded through your legs from the rear). If the opponent has his foot or feet hooked inside your legs, staying low will also make it difficult for him to lift you with elevator-type sweeps. It will be very difficult for your opponent to set up leg submissions while you are passing low. It will also be more difficult for you to set up foot locks if you

stay low and close to your opponent as you pass.

It may be more difficult to open the opponent's guard while on the knees. The opponent will be able to keep his hips on the mat for the most part, increasing his potential power, and because of your limited mobility, he will be able to adjust his position as you attempt to open his guard. Keep in mind that you can go to your feet to open the guard and then return to your knees to pass. Methods for opening the guard from standing are at the beginning of Ch. 3. But beware: Once the opponent's guard is open, if you stay on your knees he will be better able to re-lock his guard than if you are standing. This is an important consideration when fighting an opponent who prefers to attack from a closed guard.

Tournament Strategy

In competition, there are several different strategies for passing the guard. Important factors include the opponent and the circumstances. Following are some of the more common situations that occur, and some ideas on different strategies for dealing with the situations you may find yourself in. First we'll cover differences in size and physicality, and then different match situations.

Big vs. Small (Heavy vs. Light): When the opponent is larger and heavier than you, you will most likely have the advantage of speed. Very large opponents will usually not be able to move their hips as fast as smaller opponents.

If you can open the larger opponent's feet and control his legs, you will have a good chance to use speed to pass the guard. It is important to try to keep your head up and avoid letting the opponent pull your head down to his chest. Fighters with strong arms will often be able to control your head and attack.

In the open guard, stronger fighters will also be able to pull your arm in or head down for an armbar or triangle choke. Maintaining proper base, allowing you to use the power of your legs, is important for defense against a stronger opponent.

If you are heavier and stronger than your opponent, it is often easier to pass his guard by smashing him with your body weight. You will also be able to maintain strong grips and holds as you pass. With a good base, it will be harder for the smaller fighter to sweep you as you pass.

Tall vs. Short: When fighting a taller fighter, especially one with long legs, it is important to watch for armbar and triangle choke techniques. In general, it is also more difficult to break open the feet of taller fighters. Taller fighters are usually at a disadvantage when you smash their legs into their chests or over their heads.

If your opponent is shorter than you, passing under the legs is generally more difficult. Techniques that involve passing over or around the legs of shorter fighters are often easier to apply.

More Flexible vs. Less Flexible: Generally speaking, the opponent who is more flexible will have more options for attack and defense from his guard. A very flexible guard can be extremely difficult to pass.

If you can limit the mobility of the opponent's hips, you will have a better chance of passing. Also, playing a tight game, staying close to the opponent's hips and crushing him with your weight, will often prove useful against the flexible opponent.

The smash pass:

The smash pass is the first guard pass many students learn. However, it is effective at any belt level. The smash pass also opens up opportunities for other passes. Learn to use them together, and you have a guard passing game.

When you use the smash pass it is vital once you get the under-hook that you maintain constant forward pressure. Drive your opponent's knee to his face, and do not let up on the transmission of your weight through your chest as you adjust your legs during the pass.

Once the guard is open, Blue begins to reach his right arm under and around White's left leg, making sure he keeps his left elbow down against White's right leg.

Continuing, Blue presses his chest behind White's left leg, beginning to smash White's leg into his own chest. Blue stays low, making White's left leg slide onto the top of his shoulder, where he will be able to use the power of his legs and body to lift and smash the leg, rather than the power of his arm alone.

Blue will lift his knees off the mat and push off the balls of his feet in order to increase his forward power and bring more weight onto White's leg. Blue grabs inside White's right lapel with his right thumb in.

The Smash Pass

Blue breaks open White's guard...

Blue pushes off the balls of his feet.

Blue continues to smash White's leg into his chest, attempting to press White's left knee into his face as he drives forward off the balls of his feet. His legs are spread open for stability and power.

Blue makes White very uncomfortable so that White wants to take his left leg out of the way to relieve the pressure on his back. If his opponent does not take his own leg off, Blue will methodically continue with the pressure as he slowly comes further to White's side.

Forward pressure from beginning to end!

PASSING FROM THE KNEES ❖ SMASH PASS

THE KNEE-THROUGH-THE-MIDDLE (FOLLOW-UP TO THE SMASH PASS)

This technique works in combination with the smash pass on the preceding page. You use this when your opponent straight-arms your hip as you attempt to come to his side to pass (see below). Once you bring your knee through the middle, you still have the option of continuing with the smash pass if he lets go of your hip. If not, you beat his defenses by passing to his other side via the knee through the middle.

Blue begins the under-hook smash pass. White stops the pass by pushing back against Blue's hip with his left arm. Once White locks his left arm straight, it will be difficult for Blue to drop his hips and complete the pass.

Blue begins to move back around to his left and to push White's right leg to the mat.

Maintaining his forward pressure, Blue slides his left knee over the top of White's right leg. Blue slides his knee as close to White's right hip as possible.

Blue presses his weight down and under-hooks White's head with his left arm. Blue is now clear to pass to White's right side.

The Smash Pass

Blue keeps his left foot hooked over the top of White's right leg as he lifts his right leg out of the guard. If Blue takes his left hooking foot off White's right leg before he clears his right leg, White will be able to catch Blue's right leg in his half guard.

Blue whips his right leg back to the mat perpendicular to White as Blue drops his left hip to the mat. Notice that Blue keeps his weight down and head low as he passes.

Blue moves his hips toward White's head and takes his left hook off White's leg.

Blue posts on his right foot and scissors his left leg through, moving his left knee under White's right armpit into side control.

34 Passing from the Knees ◆ The Smash Pass

Stacking Pass

Good guard passing involves many factors. Sometime it is a matter of incrementally improving your position. Sometimes it is a matter of having a plan. This technique involves both.

> Sequence leading to this technique:
> 1. Blue tries to stack White's leg with the smash pass, but White makes it too heavy.
> 2. Blue attempts to pass over White's other leg, but White shifts his weight and blocks with his arm.
> 3. Now the opportunity to stack White presents itself.

Blue under-hooks White's left leg with his right arm and pushes down on the inside of White's right leg with his left hand in an attempt to pass around to White's right side.

Blue lowers his weight and drops his right shoulder as he begins to pass around White's right side. White turns onto his right hip and pushes Blue back to stop the pass.

Now that White has committed his weight to his left side, Blue has an opportunity to attack in the other direction by dropping his left knee over White's right leg.

White stiff-arms Blue's chest, stopping the knee-through-the-middle pass. When White stiff-arms, he turns off of his left side and he is no longer making his left leg heavy.

The Smash Pass

Blue already has his right arm in place as he capitalizes on the opportunity by taking a big step forward and to the side with his left foot. The forward momentum of Blue's right leg is key as it is transferred into the lifting and stacking action.

Blue circles his core to his right and slides his right shoulder underneath White's left leg as he steps.

Blue smashes his weight forward onto White, pulling with his collar-gripping right hand.

Blue moves around White's side and passes his guard.

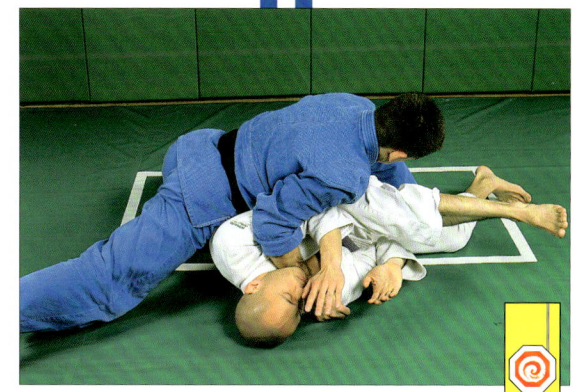

Take advantage of the moment; take one big step.

36 PASSING FROM THE KNEES ❖ THE SMASH PASS

COUNTER TO SNAKE MOVE

Sometimes your opponent will defend against the stacking game we have been looking at so far in this chapter by snaking his hips way out and getting to his side. In order to do so, he needs to push off the mat with the leg that's on the mat. As he does, there is a moment when you can easily shuffle your feet around his bottom leg. Timing is key for this one. If you wait until he finishes his snake move, he will then be able to use his bottom leg to hook your legs. You need to go when he goes. In order for that to happen, you need to be on the lookout for his snake move so you are ready when it happens.

Blue lowers his shoulders and slides White's left leg on top of his right shoulder.

Blue reaches his right hand across White's chest and grabs White's right collar with a thumb in grip.

Blue stands up in a sprawl position and drives forward off his feet.

The Smash Pass

Blue shuffles to his left and pushes White's right leg back toward his right.

Blue clears White's right leg and drives his right knee into the side of White's right hip.

Blue drops his left knee under White's right arm and completes the pass. It is important for Blue to keep constant, forward, smashing pressure with his shoulders and upper body for the duration of the pass.

Getting the opponent's leg on your shoulder

In order for the smash pass to work, there needs to be some smashing. That is not going to happen until you get the opponent's leg on your shoulder. With his leg on your shoulder, you can rely on core body strength and your legs to power your constant forward pressure.

Notice how Blue lowers his level to slide White's leg on top of his shoulder. It is important not to try to lift the opponent's leg with your arm power or from the crease of your elbow. By sliding the leg onto your shoulder, you can lift the opponent's leg with the power of your legs and hips.

Blue keeps his left elbow down and back, preventing White from pulling his arm in for a triangle.

Blue grabs White's opposite collar, thumb in. Blue sprawls his weight onto White, smashing him in preparation for the pass and maintaining constant forward pressure.

Under-hook counters

If you try to lift your opponent's legs from your elbow, not only do you waste energy, you also leave yourself open to simple counters.

As White under-hooks Blue's left leg...

Blue immediately puts his weight onto his left hip and straightens his leg a little.

Blue presses his foot to the ground to stop the pass.

The Smash Pass

Getting the Head Around the Leg

Once you smash your opponent forward, you sometimes have trouble completing your pass because his shin is on your head and neck. That is okay; to finish the pass you need to change the angle of your lower body and turn your head while maintaining forward pressure.

Blue has his right arm under-hooking White's left leg and has a grip on White's far lapel. Blue has begun to pass the guard and is smashing White with his weight.

Blue continues to move toward White's head. Blue has turned his head to look away from White's head, which helps Blue drop more of his weight into White's chest and clear his head so that White's leg will slide off his shoulder.

White's leg slips past Blue's head and Blue continues to smash his right shoulder into White's chest to complete the guard pass. Note that there is constant forward pressure on White throughout the technique.

White begins the smash pass, but he has no control over Blue's lower leg due to poor shoulder placement.

As White steps forward, Blue moves his hips back and twists onto his right hip.

Now that he has made some space, Blue hooks his left foot under White's right knee, stopping the pass.

Passing from the Knees ❖ The Smash Pass

Grips for the Smash Pass

Gripping your opponent's upper body is a vital component of the smash pass. Accordingly, your opponent may try block your grip. If you are prepared to use a variety of grips, you can improve your chances of getting a good one.

Thumb in, four fingers grip: This is the easiest grip to get. If you get it, you might be able to use the outside edge of your forearm to choke your opponent or at least to immobilize his head. Be careful not to let your opponent push the inside of your elbow. Hide it by keeping it tight to the inside.

Four fingers in: This grip prevents your opponent from pushing up on the inside of your elbow. The downside is that it is harder to grab the lapel quickly, and the grip does not lend itself well to the forearm choke.

Cup the neck: This grip works well with or without the gi. You need to reach in much deeper to establish the grip than if you grab a lapel.

Cup the far shoulder: This works well with or without the gi. You need to get your arm in very deep to make this one work. Often you will cup the neck first, adjust, and then move to this grip.

THE SMASH PASS

FOREARM CHOKE

Using the thumb-in grip with White stacked, Blue presses his right elbow toward the mat (but not all the way to it) with his wrist straight and a deep grip, crushing White's throat for the choke.

It is important for Blue to keep lifting White's hips with his left hand and pressing his weight down behind White's legs. This causes White's chest to press Blue's forearm into his neck, tightening the choke.

If White is able to take his left leg off Blue's neck, he may avoid the choke but will give up the guard pass.

METHODS FOR HOLDING AN OPPONENT IN A STACKED POSITION

Your opponent can and should try to escape the smash pass by moving his hips. You don't want that. The solution is to cage your opponent's hips so that he is prevented from moving left, right, or down. If you are exerting constant forward pressure, you probably are naturally controlling his hips fairly well. However, you may need more control than that to succeed in passing. Here are four ways to control your opponent.

Hold his belt.

Blue reaches to the far side of White's hips, grabbing his belt. Blue keeps his chest down and his weight pressing heavily on White's left leg and hips. Blue pulls up strongly on White's belt as he smashes, preventing White from recomposing his guard or rolling to his knees.

Hold his side.

Blue can accomplish the same thing by gripping the gi pants or the gi tails.

Hold his wrist.

As we will see shortly, if he can get White's wrist, a whole set of options become available.

Use the inside of your leg.

Once Blue has White stacked, he can move his left leg up behind White's hips and pinch inward to cage White's hips between his own left leg and hips. Blue can grab White's wrist for increased control as in the photos here, or he could use either of the grips above.

BREAKING DOWN STRAIGHT-ARMS:

One way your opponent may try to prevent you from passing is to straight-arm your hips to maintain space between you. If he does, you have several options for breaking through that barrier. On this page, the methods involve collapsing the opponent's elbow. On the next page the wrists are attacked, which results in the opponent collapsing his own elbows to protect his wrists.

COLLAPSE THE ELBOW FROM THE OUTSIDE.

As Blue smashes and begins to pass the guard, White pushes against Blue's hips with his left arm. Once White has locked his arm against Blue's hip, Blue will be unable to drop his hip and complete his pass.

Blue brings his right knee up and around the outside of White's left elbow.

Blue twists his hips to his left and drives his knee across White's left elbow, forcing White's arm off his hip. Blue continues to drop his weight onto his right hip and completes the pass.

COLLAPSE THE ELBOW FROM THE INSIDE

White stops the pass with the straight-arm to Blue's hip.

In this variation, Blue slides his right knee inside White's right arm above his shoulder.

Driving his hips forward, Blue forces White's hand off his hip. Continuing, Blue drops his right knee to the mat and completes the pass.

The Smash Pass

Wrist Jam
If your opponent braces against you by straight-arming you with both arms, you are not going to get anywhere by trying to power through his arms. If his hands are near your hips, use your body core against his wrists.

White blocks Blue from coming to his side by locking both his arms out at the elbows.

Blue twists his hips sharply to his left and presses down with his right hip. The pressure bends back White's wrists.

To prevent a painful wrist lock, White must bend his elbows. Then, Blue can drop down into side control.

Spin Move
These pictures are from a guard pass later in the chapter. The entry is different, but there, as here, you may wind up in a situation where you are past the legs but not the arms. The trick to everything on this spread is finding the right angle of attack to break down or move around your opponent's arms.

Kesa Gatame
Use this when your opponent's arms push straight up.

White's hands are pushing up into Blue's right hip and chest.

Blue ruins the straight arm angle by moving to the scarf hold.

Blue throws his left hip into White's left arm.

Blue's right hand pulls White's left shoulder.

Knee-on-Belly
If he straight-arms your chest, go knee-on-belly.

Palm-on-elbow counter

One way for your opponent to counter your smash pass is to push up with his palm against the elbow of your under-hooking arm. From he will try to pull back his leg, and get his knee out to the side, and push you away. You can see White attempting this in the first two frames in the photos below.

There are a couple ways to avoid this scenario entirely. The first is to keep your elbow in tight, with the point angled down, which prevents your opponent from pushing against the inside of your elbow. A second way is to use the under-hooking hand to grab the opponent's lapel with a four-fingers-in grip instead of a thumb-in grip. If you grab the lapel with a four-fingers-in grip, the point of your under-hooking elbow will automatically be down. We like the thumb-in grip because it is easier to grab, not to mention the fact that it sets you up for forearm chokes (next spread).

Blue is attempting the under-hook smash pass.

White pushes up on Blue's right elbow and slides his left knee between Blue's right arm and torso to stop the pass.

Blue goes with the force and stands.

Changing sides

Sometimes your opponent will successfully commit himself to blocking the smash pass to the side you first intended. This tends to happen when you have insufficient control over his hips. If you have your opponent folded at the waist with his knees together, you may be able switch to a thumb-in grip with your opposite hand and complete a smash pass to the other side.

Blue is attempting the under-hook smash pass around White's left side.

White shifts his hips to his left. Blue responds by reaching his left arm around White's right hip and grabbing White's left lapel.

The Smash Pass

If your opponent does get his palm into position to counter your thumb-in grip, you can counter his defense by popping up to your feet and driving a knee into his hip. That is the method shown here.

> ⊙ Driving the knee in, as Blue does below, is a valuable skill for finishing many near guard passes.

Blue begins to turn his hips to the right and slide his left knee forward, outside White's left hip.

Blue moves his left knee in front of White's left thigh.

Blue completes the pass by sliding his left shin across White's hips and controlling with the knee-on-belly position.

Blue lifts his hips in a sprawl position and drives his weight forward as he begins to move to his left.

Keeping constant forward pressure, Blue shuffles his feet around to his left as he smashes White's right leg across his body.

Blue squares his hips and completes the pass.

46 PASSING FROM THE KNEES ◆ THE SMASH PASS

UNDER-HOOK PASS WITH CHICKEN-WING VARIATION

On page 41, we recommended grabbing your opponent's wrist as part of controlling his hips. Even if you do not have his hips caged, you can use a grip on his wrist to pass guard or go to a submission. You still need to control his hips by applying constant forward pressure into his thigh, but once you get the grip you free his hips to your advantage. On this page is a smash pass variation using a wrist grip. On the next page are follow-ups using the grip.

Blue is passing the guard with the under-hook smash pass. Blue grabs deep inside White's collar with his right hand, thumb in. White leaves his right arm exposed.

Blue grabs White's wrist with his left hand.

Maintaining his forward-driving pressure, Blue pulls White's arm down below his hips.

Blue completes the pass and continues pulling White's arm up behind his back. White cannot roll away from Blue because of Blue's forearm in his throat and grip on his wrist.

The Smash Pass

Five chicken-wing continuations

1 Pushing against White's thigh with his outside leg for base and keeping his right wrist straight, Blue drives his weight into his right elbow and into White's throat for a choke.

2 Blue maintains his grip on White's wrist and pulls White's arm behind his back for the chicken-wing submission.

3 Blue slides his left palm to the back of White's wrist and pushes White's fingers toward the mat for a wrist lock.

4 Blue completes the pass and maintains his grip on White's right wrist.

Blue swings his left foot over White's hips. Blue lets go of White's wrist as he steps over.

Blue obtains the top mount.

5 Blue steps into mount.

Right away, White under-hooks.

White bridges to escape.

As Blue rolls onto his back and pulls Blue into his guard, Blue changes his grip on White's wrist from left to right.

Blue pulls his left arm out from between himself and White and reaches over White's left shoulder with his left arm.

Blue grabs White's right wrist with his left hand. Blue pulls White's arm up behind his back for the chicken-wing submission.

48 PASSING FROM THE KNEES ❖ THE SMASH PASS

PREVENTING TURTLE DEFENSES USING YOUR LEGS

A common defense to stacking-type attacks is for the bottom player to roll back over a shoulder into the turtle position. Here are two ways to use your legs to prevent a player from going to his knees.

In this situation, as Blue attempts to pass White's guard with the double under-hooks, Blue steps on White's biceps with his foot to pin down White's upper body and prevent White from turning to the turtle position.

Grabbing the cloth at White's knees, Blue bends forward and pulls White's legs off his head.

Here, as Blue attempts to pass the guard with double under-hooks, there is a lot of space. If Blue does nothing to prevent it, White is likely to attempt to go to his knees by spinning away from Blue.

Blue pulls in with the grip across White's throat as he drives his right knee forward and over White's arm. Blue drops to his knees close to White's side.

Holding himself close to White, Blue reaches up with his left hand and pulls White's legs off his head for the pass.

Knee Through the Middle Pass

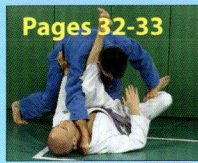      

Knee-Through-the-Middle Pass 2

On pages 32-32 (thumbnails above), we had our first look at the knee-through-the-middle pass. In that case, Blue used the knee-through-the-middle to prevent White from blocking his hips as he attempted to make the smash pass. This is a variation on that pass, only this time Blue uses the knee-through-the-middle as his first option. Instead of under-hooking with his right arm, Blue uses his forearm to block the inside of White's left leg.

Blue has opened White's guard and has grips inside both White's knees.

Blue pushes White's right knee to the mat.

Blue brings his left knee up inside his arm and over White's pinned leg.

Blue moves his hips forward and slides his left knee over the top of White's leg, as close to White's hips as possible.

Blue lowers his upper body and under-hooks White's head.

Keeping his left foot hooked over the top of White's leg to prevent White from locking Blue's right leg in the half guard, Blue whips his right leg up and back.

Blue drops his left hip to the mat with his right foot posted for stability at a 90-degree angle to White.

Posting on his right foot, Blue scissors his left leg back underneath his right.

Blue brings his right knee to White's hip. Blue obtains side control.

50   PASSING FROM THE KNEES   ◆ CROSS-KNEE PASS

CROSS-KNEE PASS (UNDER-HOOK)

The next three methods of passing allow you to use your hips to pin your opponent's hips from the top as you pass. Cross-knee passes are effective, but you need to proceed with caution. If your opponent gets to his side as you pass, the tables can quickly turn. We will see three ways to prevent this, starting with the most straight-forward: an under-hook grip to keep him flat on his back and killing his chances to escape.

Blue lifts his hips and pushes White's right knee to the mat. Blue lifts his right knee and slides it over the top of White's right leg.

Sitting on White's hips, Blue leans to his right to put all his weight on White as he reaches his right arm under White's left arm.

CROSS-KNEE PASS (OVER-HOOK)

If the guard player gets the under-hook first, you need to take different measures to keep him off his side as you pass. Here is a clever solution.

Blue breaks White's guard and begins the cross-knee pass.

Blue slides his left knee over the top of White's left upper thigh.

As Blue drives his left knee to the mat, White pummels his right arm under Blue's left arm. With the under-hook, White is in position to duck under Blue's left arm and take Blue's back.

Cross-Knee Pass

Blue lowers his upper body onto White's chest and holds tightly with his right under-hook.

Blue drops his right knee to the mat and grabs the back of White's right elbow with his left hand.

Blue pulls up strongly on White's right arm and drops his left knee, going into side control.

Blue lowers his head to the mat, tight to the left side of White's head. Blue reaches back around White's right arm and pins it to his side by holding White's belt.

Continuing, Blue grabs White's left wrist and pulls up White's arm. Blue's shoulder is on White's face and chest to keep White from circling to Blue's back.

Blue drives his hips through and finishes the guard pass.

CROSS-KNEE PASS (MARGARIDA GRIP)

It is not easy to get the under-hook against an experienced opponent. Nor is it ideal to let him have it (as in the last technique). Here is an excellent alternative to both those scenarios.

Blue opens White's guard. Blue grabs White's left lapel with a thumb-in grip and then rotates his forearm so that his left palm is turned more or less up. His right shoulder blocks the inside of White's left knee.

Blue pushes White's right knee to the mat. Blue then lifts his right knee and slides it over the middle of White's right femur, pinning White's leg.

Blue maintains his right grip on White's left lapel and drives his right elbow tightly into White's stomach. Blue's right side blocks White's left leg.

ALTERNATE BASE

Instead of finishing the pass chest-to-chest as in the examples above, Blue goes to judo base (kesa-gatame). This method allows Blue to keep weight on White's hips with his own as he finishes the pass.

This is a good option when the opponent blocks your chest with his arms. For instance, imagine if White pushed his left hand into Blue's right shoulder in the first frames.

Cross-Knee Pass

Blue lowers his upper body and slides his right knee to the mat. His right elbow comes tight to his side and his chest comes to his wrist.

Blue grabs behind White's right elbow with his left hand and pulls up strongly. This flattens White to his back.

Blue circles his left leg forward and completes the pass.

Freeing the Foot

With all of the last three guard passes, it sometimes happens that the guard player will triangle his legs around your foot in an attempt to stop the pass. Here is a solution.

Blue must be careful to keep his center of gravity off to White's right side so that White cannot reverse him.

White has triangled Blue's foot, stopping the pass.

Blue counters by pushing with his free leg against White's top knee.

Once his leg is free, Blue can easily fix his base.

54 PASSING FROM THE KNEES ❖ DOUBLE UNDER-HOOKS PASS

DOUBLE UNDER-HOOKS

The double under-hooks pass is similar to the smash pass in the way it is finished. The main difference is how it begins. Instead of under-hooking one leg with one arm, you under-hook both legs with both your arms. Instead of going straight for the collar grip as you stack your opponent, you either lock your own hands together (this spread) or hold his belt at his sides (next spread). Think about getting your opponent's hips up high and then folding them back over into his head.

Blue has already opened White's guard. Blue lowers his upper body and brings his elbows down below White's knees.

Blue wraps his arms around White's upper thighs, as close to his hips as possible. Blue locks his hands to secure the hold.

Blue drives forward off the balls of his feet and begins to push White's knees toward his head.

Continuing to smash his weight into White, Blue grabs inside White's right collar with his thumb in. Blue maintains his hold around White's right hip for control. Blue begins to circle to his right.

Blue drives his head over White's head and pushes White's legs away from him.

Blue lets go of White's collar and under-hooks his head.

Double Under-Hooks Pass

Clearing hooks

It sometimes happens that as you are fighting for the grips for the double under-hooks pass, your opponent manages to get his hooks in a space between your triceps and your thighs. Try to eliminate that space before the hooks are in. But if he does get his feet in, here is how to deal with it.

Blue sets up the double under-hook smash and pass, but White attempts to stop him by hooking his feet inside Blue's knees. With White's hooks in place, Blue is unable to lift and stack White on his shoulders.

Keeping his hips down, Blue slides his right knee back to clear White's hook. Pressure from Blue's right forearm prevents White's leg from following Blue's leg all the way back.

Blue moves his knee back and to the inside of White's left leg. To keep White from reinserting his leg, as in the first picture, Blue keeps his right elbow close to his body.

Continuing, Blue repeats the procedure on the other side, making sure to deny White the space to reinsert the hooks.

Blue now slides his left knee back up inside White's right leg. Blue is now free of White's hooks; now he can resume his pass.

Blue hops forward and brings his knees up outside White's hips. Blue crushes White's knees into his head.

Blue passes the guard and establishes side control.

56 PASSING FROM THE KNEES ❖ DOUBLE UNDER-HOOKS PASS

DOUBLE UNDER-HOOKS 2 (THE RAMP)

On the previous spread, Blue drove his shoulders into White's legs and then hopped to his feet, which helped him get a better angle to stack White's hips toward White's head. That method is more susceptible to White defending by putting his hooks in (also on the previous spread). This time, Blue keeps things tighter by dragging White's hips back and up. Blue uses the tops of his thighs like a ramp to elevate and control White's hips.

Blue breaks White's guard and holds the outsides of his hips with both hands.

Blue will use his thighs like a ramp to slide White's hips up. Blue locks his hands around White's thighs near his hips and pulls.

Blue pulls White's hips toward himself so that White slides up with his hips resting on top of Blue's thighs.

Now that their hips are connected, Blue puts the balls of his feet on the mat and uses them for base as he drives forward.

Double Under-Hooks Pass

Blue grabs inside White's right collar deep as possible with his right hand, thumb in.

Keeping a tight grip around White's legs, Blues comes off his knees and steps his right leg off to the side. Notice how the right side of his pelvis dips as he does. This allows him to stay tight while driving into White's side.

From here, the situation is the same as with the smash pass.

Blue wraps his right arm over the top of White's left shoulder and then behind White's head. This prevents White from turning away and going into the turtle position.

ALTERNATIVE SMASH PASS GAME--SMASH PASS

Controlling the upper part of an opponent's leg gives you some control over their hips. The next few techniques are premised on controlling one of your opponent's upper legs by trapping it in a triangle formed by your arm, your side, and your leg. Done correctly, this method allows you to swim your other arm in for the under-hook with little danger of being triangled or attacked with an armbar.

Blue locks down White's left knee by clamping his elbow down on the outside of his thigh and crunching his abs a bit.

Being careful to keep White's left knee trapped, Blue begins working for the under-hook. The point of his left elbow pushes inside White's right knee.

Blue drops weight onto his left elbow. He only needs a small opening for his bladed hand to slip through.

Blue's left shoulder drops to the inside of White's right knee and breaks open the guard. Blue still has control of White's left leg.

SHIN GRAB METHOD OF GETTING THE UNDER-HOOK

One of the advantages of the smash pass shown above over those shown earlier in the chapter is that you do not need to break open your opponent's legs to begin the pass. All you need to do is make enough space to work your arm through, and that does not require much space at all. Once your arm is through, you may not find yourself at a good angle for getting the opponent's leg on your shoulder where you want it. Here, then, is a solution to that problem. Note that you can also use the method below with the smash passes from earlier in the chapter.

White has his guard closed tightly. Blue establishes his base.

Blue moves his left leg back and begins to insert his left hand inside White's right leg.

Blue straightens his left arm and works on grabbing his left shin.

Blue lowers his body and grabs the front of his left shin with his left hand.

Alternative Smash Pass Game

Blue gets his left shoulder all the way behind the back of White's upper leg, just like with the regular smash pass. Blue makes a deep thumb-in grip on White's lapel.

Blue still has tight control on White's left leg. Blue drives forward, first off his left foot.

Only now that he has White's right knee smashed forward does Blue partially release White's left leg. But when he does, he immediately uses his right forearm to block the inside of White's right leg.

Blue circles his feet while smashing his knee into White's face until he gets to the side and clears White's right leg.

With both of these techniques you must control the opponent's upper leg solidly with one arm before you make the under-hook with the other. Hold their leg in a triangle formed by your thigh, stomach, and upper arm. It is not a closed triangle, like with the triangle choke. Instead, you must overlap your elbow to the outside of your thigh and keep it tight. Make cross-pressure on his femur by dropping your side and triceps near the opponent's knee, and pushing their femur up with the top of your thigh near your knee. Essentially you are using your knee as a fulcrum to lift one side of his hips, and his upper knee area as the lever. The pressure is like the pressure you make when applying the standard armbar (juji-gatame). This pressure controls their hips and prevents triangle and armbar attacks until it is too late for him.

Blue moves his left knee forward and uses the leverage of his leg to aid his arm in breaking White's guard.

Blue drives his left shoulder forward behind White's right thigh and reaches for White's left lapel with his left hand.

Blue grabs inside White's left collar with his left hand, thumb in, as he moves around to his left. Notice Blue keeps his hips low and his weight pushing down and forward into White.

Blue drives his hips down and passes the guard.

Alternative Smash Pass Game—Pass the Low Leg

In order to defend the last technique, your opponent may defend by snaking his hips out toward your under-hooking arm, preventing you from stacking his leg. When he does, his other leg will turn sideways. Because it is sideways, an opportunity opens to pass over his free leg by pinning it down at the knee with your torso or by hopping over it.

Blue attempts the previous under-hook pass.

As Blue begins to under-hook White's right leg and pass, White begins to move his hips back.

White snakes his hips back, preventing Blue from passing under White's right leg. Notice the position of White's left knee. It is straight and to the side. If Blue can pin it in this position, he has a good route to pass.

Alternative Smash Pass Game

In order to move his hip away, White must turn his left hip down. Taking advantage of this, Blue immediately sprawls his hips back and smashes White's left leg to the mat with his right hip. Blue drives forward as he sprawls and smashes White's leg.

Keeping his weight down, Blue maintains his left under-hook control over White's right leg as he hooks White's head with his right arm.

Blue shuffles on the balls of his feet toward his right side, passing the guard.

This is a way to get around your opponent's hook if you can keep his knee pinned sideways.

Blue sprawls on White's left leg and begins the pass. White attempts to stop the pass by hooking his left foot over the top of White's left leg.

Keeping White's left leg pinned to the ground with his hips, Blue bends his knee and hooks the top of his foot over the top of White's left ankle, clearing the hook.

Blue continues and passes the guard.

ALTERNATIVE SMASH PASS GAME—SCISSORS GUARD

One of the most common and effective guard recomposition techniques is for the guard player to turn to his side and bring his knee in front of the passer's chest. We call this position the scissors guard.

The technique on this spread is a third move in the alternate smash pass game of the last four pages. It is also the beginning of another game for dealing with the scissors guard.

Blue breaks the guard and begins to pass.

White moves his hips away to make space and prevent the pass.

White turns onto his left hip and slides his right shin across the front of Blue's chest in the scissors guard.

Blue reaches between White's legs and hooks the palm of his left hand over the top of White's left thigh. Blue also grabs outside White's left elbow with his right hand.

Keeping the weight of his upper body pressing down on White's upper body, Blue lifts his hips a little and begins to shuffle to his right.

Blue shuffles toward his right on the balls of his feet. At the same time, Blue pushes back against White's left thigh as he pulls up on White's left arm.

Scissors Pass #1

Blue pushes White's right knee down with his left hand.

Blue now drops his chest on top of the outside of White's right leg. Notice Blue has moved forward and his head is low.

Blue clears White's feet and underhooks White's head. Note how he forces White to look at the ceiling; this prevents White from continuing to turn into Blue.

Blue drives his left knee up into White's left hip and establishes side control.

Re: Gripping

This is an example of a bad grip on the leg. White is grabbing the cloth instead of over the top of the thigh.

Because of the slack in the cloth, Blue is able to extend his right leg ...

... and snap off White's grip.

SCISSORS PASS 2

If you were simply to attempt the previous pass without any contingency plans, it might not serve you well. Your opponent has options and counters of his own. But they are predictable. If you understand them and know their counters, you have the upper hand. Here then, and over the next several spreads, we will look at various contingency plans covering the most likely reactions from your opponent as you attempt to pass the scissors guard.

Blue attempts to pass the scissors guard.

Defending, White brings his top knee up high to block the pass.

Keeping his hips and weight down, Blue turns his left hand palm upward (Blue's left hand was holding over the top of White's left thigh) and grabs around the front of White's top (right) thigh. Because White's top leg is blocking Blue, Blue must get it out of the way.

Let's look again from another angle: Blue attempts to pass the scissors position, but White brings his top leg high to block.

Blue changes his grip to a palm-up hold on the top of White's right thigh.

Blue lifts his hips a little and pulls White's right leg back out of the way.

Blue slides his right knee in and passes the guard.

Scissors Pass #2

Keeping his head and chest down, Blue lifts his hips slightly and pulls White's right thigh back to clear the leg.

As soon as Blue pulls White's top leg back and out of the way, he brings his left knee up against White's left hip.

Once Blue slips in his left knee, White no longer has space to replace the guard. Blue under-hooks White's head and comes to side control.

If Your Opponent Pushes Up…

Blue is attempting to pass the scissors position, but White pushes his upper body away, preventing him from putting his weight down to pass.

Blue turns his hips so that he leads with his left hip as White pushes up his chest.

Blue takes advantage of the space and slides his left knee across White's hips for the knee on belly position.

> ⊙ The defense White uses above occurs with a variety of guard passes. Regardless of how you get there, if your opponent defends by pushing up, switch to the knee-on-the-belly position.

SCISSORS PASS 3: REVERSE

Sometimes, when you pull back on your opponent's top leg from the scissors guard, he will react by bringing his bottom leg under (as in the first two pictures of each sequence below). This creates a simple, efficient opportunity for you to pass, but only if you seize the moment when it comes. So be ready!

Once again, Blue attempts to pass the scissors position. This time, however, White will defend against Blue pulling back his top leg. As Blue pulls ...

... White attempts to twist his hips, bring his bottom leg through, and put Blue back into the guard. As on the preceding page, Blue has changed his left grip to hold White's top leg and has pulled it back to make space to pass.

Because White is countering by bringing his lower leg back through, Blue uses the moment to reverse his direction of attack. Keeping the weight of his upper body down, he jumps over White's legs to his rear. He keeps his left shoulder and head pushing down on White's hips as he springs over to keep White from hooking his leg.

> ⦿ Timing is key. Blue's jump must coincide with White's attempt to bring his bottom leg under to fix his position.

Here is a view from the other side. Note the placement of Blue's hands. This move requires sensitivity to White's movement.

As White tries to bring his bottom leg under to stop the pass, Blue must simultaneously spring himself the other way. As he jumps, his body weight transfers from his left shoulder into White's right leg, preventing White from hooking with it.

Scissors Pass #3

> ◉ This pass requires little strength, but a measure of agility.

Blue balance on the balls of his feet with his legs apart for better base in a sprawl position behind White.

Blue has control of White's far (left) arm, so it is unlikely White will be able to turn to his knees. Blue moves toward White's head and applies weight with his chest.

Blue's left arm lets go of White's leg and Blue uses it to control White's head.

From here, Blue has all but completed the pass.

If possible, Blue will bring his left arm to the inside of White's right so that Blue's left arm is over White's shoulder and under White's head, preventing White from turning away and going to the turtle position.

Scissors Pass 4A: Step-over to Mount

On page 63 we recommended going to the knee-on belly position if, as you are coming to the side, your opponent tries to deflect your upper body upward. He might also stiff-arm you off to his side. If so, consider this move.

Blue attempts to pass the scissors position, but White straight-arms Blue's shoulder. Blue is using his left arm to pin down White's right knee so that White cannot use it to fix his guard. Blue's right hand is holding White's left arm; if it was not, White could pull his left arm through and go to the turtle position.

Blue switches his hips so that he can hook his right instep over White's right knee.

Blue puts most of his weight on White's trapped right knee as he steps over. As he steps over, his left arm reaches around White's upper back.

Scissors Pass 4B: Step-over to Side Control

Here is the pass from the other side, ending in side control instead of the mount. Once again, White maintains space by straight-arming Blue's shoulder/chest.

Blue holds the top of White's right leg, drops his left hip, and scissors his left foot through, pressing his left ankle over the top of White's left shin or knee.

Scissors Pass #4

Blue puts his left knee behind White's lower back. From here, Blue has the option of going to the mount or continuing to circle around to White's back, which would allow him to move to side control.

If Blue wants the mount, he will stretch out White's upper body by moving back White's head.

Blue locks his hands as he stretches White's head and puts him on his back for the mount.

◀ If Blue goes for side control, he must do something to prevent White from rolling away from him into the turtle position. This time, Blue stops that by controlling White's bottom (left) arm. Blue might also use one of the other options shown on pgs. 86-87.

Blue swings his right foot over White while smashing his weight down. Blue's right leg hooks White's hips.

Blue hugs White tightly with his right arm as he shifts his weight over the top of White's hips, putting his right knee down behind White.

Blue swings his right leg over to White's rear and comes to side control. To keep White from going to his knees, Blue must keep good control. Here, Blue hugs the head and arm.

SCISSORS PASSES 5A-C: STEP-OVER TO MOUNT OR SIDE CONTROL

The situation this time is that Blue has gotten around White's legs and has closed the space between their upper bodies. White is using his top (right) knee to stop Blue from moving in and establishing control. Unlike in the last spread, Blue is not being straight-armed. Also, Blue's hip is on the mat, whereas in the previous technique Blue's hips did not touch the mat. Blue's legwork in the three variations here involves him hooking his top (left) leg over White's leg after he first drops to his

Blue attempts the scissors pass. White attempts to block the pass by bringing his right knee up high in front of Blue's chest.

Maintaining his left grip on White's right leg, Blue begins to twist his hips to his left.

Blue scissors his right knee through as he sits on his right hip.

Once again, Blue is to White's side, but White defends by staying to his side, using his right knee to block Blue's hips.

Blue keeps hold of White's top leg as he drops to his right side. Blue hooks his left foot over the top of White's right ankle.

Now Blue hooks his right ankle over the top of White's knee.

The sequence begins just like the two above.

SCISSORS PASS #5

right side. If White tries to turn to his back, White pulls Blue into the mount. In the second and third variations, Blue uses his left leg to briefly hold White's top (right) leg in place while he hooks his right instep over White's top (right) knee, just as in the last spread. Once again, Blue climbs over, using that instep for base, and once again Blue has the option of transitioning to mount or side control.

Blue hooks his left foot over the top of White's right ankle.

White pulls his right leg back, Blue pulls with his left hook, and White literally pulls Blue to the top mount.

Blue establishes the top mount position.

Blue kicks his left leg over White's hips. Notice Blue has his weight down.

Blue moves forward, sliding his right leg up over White's right leg.

Blue moves into top mount.

▲▼ To this point, both are the same.

Blue lifts himself up and over, using his right instep against the outside of the bend in White's leg as a point of base.

This time there is not enough space between White's top (right) knee and his shoulders for Blue to transition to the mount. Blue counters by moving to White's back.

Blue moves to side control. Blue is ready with the techniques from pgs. 86-87 should White try to escape by rolling away from Blue and going to his knees.

72 Passing from the Knees ❖ Scissors Pass #6

Scissors Pass 6: Flip and Turn

If your opponent does a good job of preventing you from finishing your guard pass by blocking with his top knee and arm, consider this technique. This one is particularly good if he straight-arms the top of your head and tries to push it down to the mat. This one looks more difficult than it is. The tricky part to this pass is not the flip over; it is the ensuing scramble. If your opponent's arm winds up hooked under yours after you flip and turn, he will not be able to escape to his hands and knees, so that is what you want. Otherwise, after you flip and turn, immediately look for another method of keeping him from turning over using one of the techniques from pgs. 86-87.

White defends his guard by pushing Blue's shoulder (or head, as the case may be) and blocking with his top (right) knee, preventing Blue from moving in for side control.

Blue ducks his head down and posts the top of his head on the mat in front of White's chest.

Posting off his head, Blue kicks his feet up and over White.

❷ Blue threads his left arm in front of White's right shoulder and then behind White's head so that White cannot escape to the turtle position. See pages 86-87 for more technique to prevent your opponent from going to his hands and knees.

Scissors Pass #6

> 🌀 Note the position of Blue's left leg after he lands on his feet. His left leg does not step over his right leg; his right leg goes under a "bridge" created by his left leg as his hips turn to the mat. If you do not do it this way, when you turn over you will wind up with your torso above your opponent's head, and he will escape.

Maintaining his grips on White's leg and arm, Blue lands in the bridge position over White.

Blue keeps his weight on top of White, releases his left grip, twists his hips to the right, and scissors his right leg through to the rear. Note the position of Blue's left leg after he lands on his feet. His left leg does not step over his right leg; his right leg goes under a "bridge" created by his left leg. Blue pulls his right leg back.

Blue establishes side control.

Here is a better look at how Blue threads his arm over White's shoulders and behind his head.

Passing from the Knees ❖ Scissors Pass #7

Foot trap scissors pass

Here is another scissors guard pass. This time you still must smash down your opponent's top knee, but instead of wrapping up his thigh to control his top leg, you trap his heel to his butt with the aid of their gi. If you can immobilize one of your opponent's arms using one of your arms, there is a good chance there is a guard pass to be had, and that is case here. Look for this move when the instep of your opponent's scissoring top leg is not flush to your hip. If it is not, it will be easier to get your arm in front of it to trap the leg.

White turns onto his right side and slides his right shin across Blue's hips in the scissors sweep position. Blue smashes White's knee by dropping his chest on it. Maintaining his grip, Blue moves his hips back a little and lowers his weight.

Blue drops his chest on the outside of White's right leg, smashing it into White's left (bottom) leg. He holds White's left elbow with his right hand. Blue reaches behind White's right ankle with his left hand.

Blue reaches up and grabs White's belt, trapping White' right foot against his rear.

Scissors Pass #7

Blue sprawls, smashing both White's legs down against the mat. Blue wants White's trapped right foot to be a little higher than White's right knee. This helps immobilize White.

Keeping his weight on top of White's legs, Blue posts on the balls of his feet and begins to circle to White's front. He moves his right hand over White's shoulder as he goes.

Blue shuffles his feet around to his left, clearing White's legs. Blue then reaches behind White's neck and moves his left knee against White's left hip, coming to side control.

LOW MOUNT

We put this technique here because it does present itself sometimes when you are attempting to pass the scissors guard and wind up using both your arms to control your opponent's legs. There are many other ways you could get here, while attempting the lasso pass from page 144 for instance. However you get there, you find yourself with his legs wrapped up, but he is blocking you from controlling his upper body by blocking your shoulder and/or head with his palms or elbows. Turn him to a side so that your head can go off to the top side and then switch control over his legs from your arms to your legs. Now you use your arms to help climb up his upper body. You may have to inch your way up to succeed. If so, keep your ankles crossed and keep his knees pinned together by making pressure with the insides of your knees as you go.

While passing to White's left side, Blue hugs around both of White's legs and squeezes tightly above White's knees.

Blue steps his left leg over White's lower legs.

Blue scoops back White's legs, bringing his right foot under his left. Blue drives White to his back.

Blue crosses his ankles and brings his weight down on the top of White's knees.

Blue begins crawling up toward White's head. He shimmies up, like he is climbing a tree. Blue seems to progress up in one big move in the photos, but in reality he may have to battle for an inch at a time. Blue keeps White's knees fully extended as he goes by pushing down with his hips.

Once Blue's upper body is over White's upper body, Blue slides his knees up to the top mount.

SIMPLE HOPPING PASS

Many of the techniques so far have involved smashing the opponent's legs with sustained constant pressure. Sometimes, however, you only need to hold them down for a moment as you make a timed move. This is one such technique.

Here, you push down on your opponent's knee to momentarily stick his foot to the mat at the same time that you hop over that leg.

Blue holds inside White's right leg with his left hand, grabbing the cloth thumb down.

Blue lowers his torso and rolls his right arm underneath White's left leg. It is important to lower the body as you wrap the arm in order to hold the opponent's leg close to your shoulder.

Blue pushes down with his left arm, turns his head to the right, and smashes his left shoulder into White's hips.

Blue pushes off his left-hand grip as he sprawls his leg and throws his hips over White's right knee. Next, he shuffles his feet as necessary. As Blue shuffles his feet, he does not take the forward pressure off of White's hips, and his feet do not cross.

Once Blue has cleared White's right leg, he drives his right knee up against White's right hip.

Blue under-hooks White's head with his left arm and establishes side control.

In the sequence above, Blue hooked his right arm under White's right leg as he hopped over White's left leg. This time, Blue holds White's pants and pushes down White's right knee. The rest of the technique is the same.

SHOULDER PLANT

Sometimes you will need, or want, to jump higher than the simple hopping pass (previous page). Usually you will do so in a situation where your opponent has a hook, but you know that he cannot follow you with the hook as far as you can elevate your hips. When you do have to jump higher, the better practice is to post off the foot on the side you are jumping to, lifting the foot opposite the side you are jumping to first. On the way down, the leg that went up first, comes down first, and that knee moves to the opponent's hip right away. This is how Blue jumps in the technique here.

Blue opens White's guard on his knees. Blue grabs inside White's left knee with his left hand, the thumb pointing backward. Blue also under-hooks White's left leg with his left hand.

Blue looks to his right and lowers his left shoulder on top of White's pelvis.

Blue shifts his weight to his left shoulder and begins to lift his hips.

Pushing off with his left foot, Blue swings his right leg into the air.

Continuing the momentum, Blue swings his left leg into the air and begins to turn in a clockwise circle to his left.

Shoulder Plant

Blue continues his rotation in the air until his body is perpendicular to White's.

Blue drops onto his feet and knees at White's left side.

Blue lands with his knees close to White's left side and hip.

Blue reaches his left arm around and under-hooks White's neck.

Blue establishes side control.

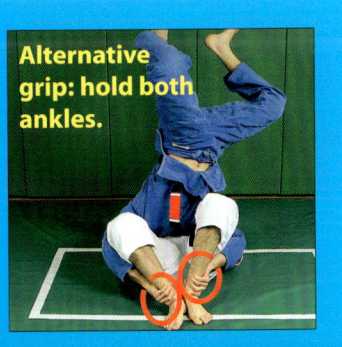  

Alternative grip: hold both ankles.

Leg Trap Pass 1

A good strategy for passing the guard is to trap one of your opponent's legs between your legs and keep the other to the outside. You take away a lot of your opponent's offense while establishing control over one of his legs. The next three techniques are applications of this strategy.

Blue has opened White's guard.

Blue under-hooks White's right leg with his left hand and grabs outside White's left knee with his right hand.

Pushing down on White's left knee, Blue lifts his left foot and begins to turn his hips to his left.

Blue's hips clear White's left knee as he drops his left foot back to the mat.

Leg Trap Passes

Maintaining his grips, Blue slides his right leg back.

Blue slides his right knee back up on the outside of White's left foot.

Blue lays his upper body weight down, turning his head to his left and pressing down heavily with his right shoulder.

> ⊚ Be careful about leaving your arm between your opponent's legs anytime you pass. There is a danger that he will push your head toward his feet and throw on a reverse triangle choke with his legs.

Posting on his left foot, Blue scissors his right knee through to his right.

Blue brings his knees up and underhooks White's head with his right arm.

Blue pulls his left arm out from between White's legs and establishes side control.

Leg trap pass 2

Blue opens White's guard and grabs inside White's right knee with his left hand and outside White's left knee with his right hand.

Blue slides his right leg back as he pushes White's left knee forward.

Blue slides his right knee up against White's left shin, and traps White's left heel against his rear.

Blue drives his weight forward and puts his weight on his right knee.

Blue slides his left leg back.

Blue slides his left knee up next to his right knee and holds White's left foot against his rear. Both Blue's knees are pressed against White's right shin at this point.

LEG TRAP PASSES

Blue hugs White's neck with his right arm and reaches back with his left hand.

Blue hooks his left arm over the top of White's left ankle and grabs underneath White's hips to secure White's left foot against his hips.

Blue drops his right hip over White's left knee and to the mat.

Blue kicks his left leg back over his right leg. Blue keeps his left grip in place and his weight down.

Posting on his left foot, Blue lifts his hips.

Blue scissors his right knee back under his left and moves into side control.

◀ Note how Blue traps White's instep with his left hand. His forearm is across White's instep, pinning White's foot. Blue's hand grips near White's hip or rear.

LEG TRAP PASS 3

If you can get both your opponent's feet to one side of your body while passing from the knees, this is another option for controlling his legs as you pass.

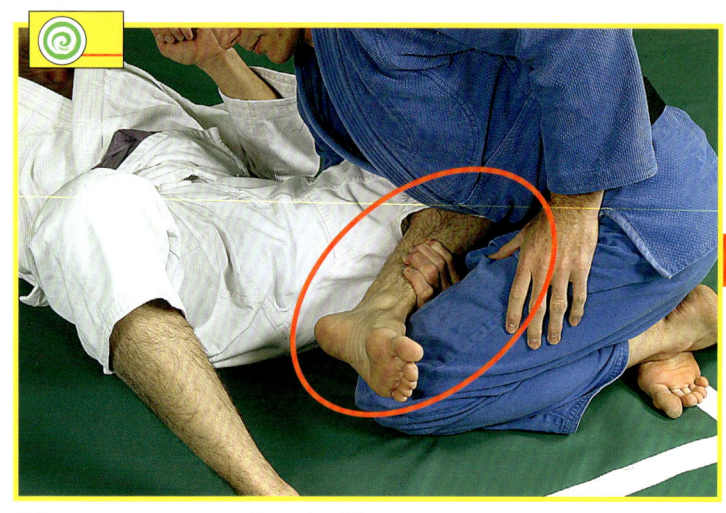

Here, you can see the grip Blue uses to pass White's legs in the next two photos.

ONE LEG AT A TIME

If your opponent has one or both hooks in, most of the time in order to jump or hop to the side of your opponent's legs, you need to do something to stop him from following you with his hooks. As we saw in the last several techniques, there are various ways you can use your hands to do so. If you are bent forward and have your hands on your opponent's hips, another way to trap the leg is to use the triceps or the back of your upper arm. You could also just rely on the element of surprise, which is what Blue is attempting in the first four frames

Blue holds White on his back. White has both feet hooked inside Blues' legs.

Blue lifts his hips and begins the jumping pass without first securing White's feet.

Blue kicks up his right leg.

Blue swings up his left leg and starts to turn to his left in the air. Because White's legs are free, he follows Blue's hips with his left leg.

LEG TRAP PASSES

Instead of trapping White's left foot with his left arm, Blue can also under-hook White's right hip with his left arm.

Blue lifts his hips and shuffles around to his right to clear White's knee and pass the guard.

of the photo sequences below. Sometimes, however, you will not get past his legs on your first try, as is the case below. If, as you hop, you can get rid of one of your opponent's hooks, so that one of his legs is to the outside, you are making progress, particularly if you can get his instep to the outside of both your legs (fifth frame). From there, you can use any of the last three techniques to complete the guard pass.

As Blue lands, he cannot complete the pass because White's left shin is across Blue's hips.

Blue has obtained a superior angle. He immediately sprawls his legs back and smashes his hips on top of White's left leg, pinning the leg to the mat.

Blue puts his right palm on top of White's left thigh and lifts his hips.

Blue pushes White's left thigh to the left, below his hips, slides his left knee against the side of White's left hip, and comes into side control.

BRIDGING PASS

If your legs are free and your opponent's guard is open, flipping over him becomes an option. On this spread are two flipping guard passes. With either flip, it is crucial that you land on your feet so that your butt does not hit on the landing. Also, as with some of the previous guard passes, when you turn over you must not roll past your opponent's head. You can prevent that by bringing one leg under the other as you turn. Getting good at the drills on pgs. 299 and 302 will help you with this.

Blue is in White's open guard. Blue posts his left palm on the mat between White's legs. With his right hand, Blue grabs inside White's left knee, grabbing the cloth thumb down.

Blue lays his right shoulder on top of White's hips and turns his head to the left. Blue posts on the balls of his feet.

Pushing off with his right foot, Blue swings his left leg straight up to his rear. As his left foot goes vertical, Blue follows by swinging his right foot up beside his left.

Blue lands in a bridge with his feet above White's left shoulder.

Blue releases his right grip and begins to turn to his left.

Blue twists his body to the left, letting go of White's leg, and slides his left foot back for base. Blue puts his left arm down on the mat at White's right side.

SOMERSAULT PASS

In this variation of the technique above, Blue puts his head down between White's legs instead of posting his shoulder on White's hips. It is easier to keep from rolling past White's head this way.

FLIPPING PASSES

87

Blue lands in a bridge, feet on the opposite side of White's head.

Blue lands on the balls of his feet, in a bridge.

Maintaining his grip on White's left leg with his right hand, Blue turns over, kicking his left foot over his right and posting his left hand outside White's right side.

Blue lets go of White's leg with his right arm and under-hooks White's head for side control.

Blue scissors his left leg back under his right and under-hooks White's head with his right arm, establishing side control.

PASSING FROM THE KNEES ❖ SPIN PASSES

SPIN PASS

It is one thing to get past the legs and another to pass the guard. Some guard passes are great for getting past the legs but don't account for being straight-armed. If your opponent's arms are blocking your hips, you won't get anywhere by pushing directly into them. Try rolling over you opponent's hands. As your weight goes over his fingers, his wrist will get locked backwards and he will collapse his elbows to protect his wrists.

Blue attempts to pass with the shoulder smash pass. White pushes against Blue's right hip with his arms locked, preventing the pass.

Posting on his right foot, Blue turns his hips to his left and whips his left leg back over the top of his right leg. Notice that Blue keeps his upper body weight down as he twists his hips.

Blue posts his left foot on the mat and lowers his hips.

Continuing the spin, Blue twists his shoulders to his left and swings his left arm back toward White's head. Blue keeps his upper body weight on White's chest as much as possible.

Continuing the spin, Blue twists his chest down and under-hooks White's head with his right arm.

Blue maintains head control and keeps his upper body weight down on White as he scissors his left leg back under his right, coming to the side control position.

❷ Pit your weight and the strength of your torso against your opponent's wrists. As the spin begins, you must step back under your hips with your front foot, or switch the position of your feet, so that you do not spin past your opponent's head.

Sitting Guard Passes

BASIC SITTING GUARD DEFENSE:
In *Strategic Guard,* there are a couple chapters concerning sitting guard. Over the next five pages, we look at techniques for countering and passing the sitting guard. Techniques require positioning. That goes for both players all the time. If you know the elements your opponent needs for a given attack, you can prevent it by disrupting one or more of its elements. Keep that in mind when confronted with attacks that are new to you. On this page is but one example of taking away elements to prevent an attack.

White sits up with both feet hooked inside Blue's legs. White slides his left arm under Blues' right arm and buries his head below Blue's chin.

Blue moves his head back, lowers his upper body, and drives his head underneath White's head. At the same time, Blue pummels his right arm underneath White's left arm. Blue has denied White both the under-hook and the head position he needs for most of his attacks.

Blue drives forward and pins White flat on his back.

PASSING FROM THE KNEES ❖ PASSING SITTING GUARD

BODY-LOCK PASS

White sits up and fixes the butterfly guard position.

Blue grabs behind White's left shoulder with his right hand and pulls his elbow in tightly. At the same time, Blue grabs outside White's right knee with his left hand and, turning his hips to his right, pushes White's right knee down to Blue's right.

Continuing, Blue sprawls his legs back and smashes his upper body on the outside of White's right leg, pinning White's legs together on the mat.

This technique can start from standing or the knees. By smashing one of your opponent's legs on top of the other, you pin both. By controlling the arm opposite his top knee, which you have smashed in front of his bottom knee, you prevent him from going belly-down. The basic idea is to put a twist in his torso to immobilize him. You want your opponent on his side so that his top leg is in front of his bottom leg. If his top leg is behind his bottom leg, it is easy for him to turn his back to the mat and, at the least, get to half-guard. If his top knee is in front of the bottom knee and you drop your hips into his top leg, his top leg becomes a barrier to his bottom leg; that is what you want. Then, with control of his opposite arm, you will be in a position to use your instep to step behind his knee and either circle behind him to side control or climb forward to mount.

> More body lock style passes at pgs. 134-137, Ch. 3.

Passing Sitting Guard

Blue begins to shuffle his feet and move around to his right side. Blue must keep his weight smashing heavily downward on White's legs and a firm grip on White's left shoulder with his right hand.

Keeping his weight down, Blue hooks the top of his right ankle over the top of White's right ankle to control White's legs.

Blue slides his left knee up behind White's shoulders and continues to move around to his right side, passing the guard.

Transition to the Mount

From the same pass, after smashing White's legs together, Blue can also drive his left knee between White's crossed legs.

Pulling up on White's left arm, Blue keeps his weight down and slides his body up toward White's head.

As White attempts to right himself by turning onto his back, he pulls Blue to the top mount position.

PASSING FROM THE KNEES ❖ PASSING SITTING GUARD

PASSING SITTING GUARD
Sitting guard with an under-hook is a great position for initiating sweeps. All positions have their relative strengths and weaknesses. Here are three ways to undermine the sitting guard position by using the under-hook against the opponent.

Blue is in the butterfly guard. Blue moves to his left, grabs over the top of White's left shoulder with his right hand, and grabs inside White's left ankle with his left hand.

Blue lowers his head and presses it into White's chest.

Blue drives forward into White and begins to lift White's left leg.

In the same situation as above, Blue grabs over the top of White's left shoulder with his right hand and lowers his head into White's chest.

This time, Blue's grip is different. Instead of grabbing White's left ankle with his left hand, Blue reaches around the outside of White's right ankle and grabs the cloth behind White's left ankle.

Blue falls back onto his right side as before.

In this variation, Blue over-hooks White's left arm with his right arm and grabs his own left lapel as he moves to his right.

Blue pulls his left knee back and clears White's right hook.

Blue sits back and slides his right knee under White's left leg.

Passing Sitting Guard

Blue lifts his left knee up to clear White's right hook as he lies down on his right side. By lying on his side, Blue will also clear White's left hook. As soon as his right leg is clear, Blue lifts White's left foot up for control.

Blue lifts his hips off the mat and maintains control of White's left ankle.

Blue scissors his right leg back toward White's head and moves into side control.

Blue pulls up on White's left ankle and clears his right leg.

Blue continues pulling up on White's legs as he lifts his hips.

Blue scissors his right leg back toward White's head and completes the pass.

Blue's right shin/foot can block or follow White's lifted left foot any way White can move it. Blue lies on his back and lifts White's left leg with his left shin/knee.

To prevent White from following him up and achieving side control, Blue under-hooks White's left leg with his left arm and lifts White's leg.

Blue lifts his hips and scissors his right leg back toward White's head, moving into side control.

OPPONENT ROLLS AWAY FROM YOU:

We switch focus now and deal with some problems that arise when passing the guard generally. One of the best methods for preventing a guard pass is to go to the turtle position. In judo, it is done all the time. In jiu-jitsu, some players do this all the time and some are averse to it, usually because they are not good from this position. Here, we look at various methods for keeping the opponent from going belly-down. These methods come in handy with a variety of guard passes and also against escapes from side control.

Blue grabs White's collar with his right hand. His right elbow drops as he drives his forearm into White's neck. The pressure to his neck stops White from turning further.

Blue figure-fours White's top arm and drops his butt.

Blue hugs behind White's bottom arm with both hands.

Blue hugs behind White's neck with his right arm and under his right arm with his left.

Blue inserts his arm in front of White's left shoulder and under-hooks White's head.

Turtle Prevention

OPPONENT ROLLS AWAY FROM YOU:
This is a good option if you are too late to use one of the techniques on the last page or as a first option. As your opponent goes to his knees, he will lift his hips. When he does, there will be space for you to slide your bottom leg between his legs. At the same time, you grab under his top shoulder and over his bottom shoulder and then clasp your hands. The position achieved is known as the harness grip. The harness grip gives you diagonal control over his torso and diagonal control from the back, which is hard to escape. The intricacies of the harness grip are beyond this volume, but one of the primary options is to take the back.

As Blue passes White's guard, White turns onto his right side.

White kicks his left leg over and attempts to go to the turtle position. Blue hooks over White's left hip with his left hand.

Blue posts his left foot on the mat and starts to pull back on White's hip.

Blue lies on his right hip and slides his right knee under White's right hip and between White's legs.

Blue hooks his right arm over the top of White's right shoulder.

Blue locks his hands in the over-and-under grip from the rear as he hooks his left leg over the top of White's right leg. Blue crosses his ankles and scissors White's right leg. Blue now has excellent control over White's movement.

Blue pulls upward with his arms and shucks White upward as Blue slides his hips downward.

Leaving his right hook over White's right hip, Blue unlocks his feet.

Blue hooks his left foot over White's left hip to complete taking the back.

Passing from the Knees ❖ Turtle Prevention

Opponent rolls into you:

To get to the turtle position, your opponent might also roll into you. This is less frequent than him turning away, because it is harder for your opponent to find the space to make it happen. You don't have as many options as when he rolls away, but the option you do have, cross-facing your opponent, is a good one. Even if it does not keep him on his back, your opponent will tend to set himself up for a choke, the clock choke for example.

The problem:

As Blue comes around to White's right side during a guard pass...

...White begins turning to his right.

White moves onto all fours in the turtle position.

The solution:

Blue is passing to White's right side.

White begins to turn into Blue and escape to his knees. Blue immediately grabs the right side of White's collar with his left hand, with a thumb-in grip. When it comes to the cross-face, the deeper the grip is behind the neck, the better.

Blue drives his forearm into either White's neck or his face. Either way, White is forced from his side to his back.

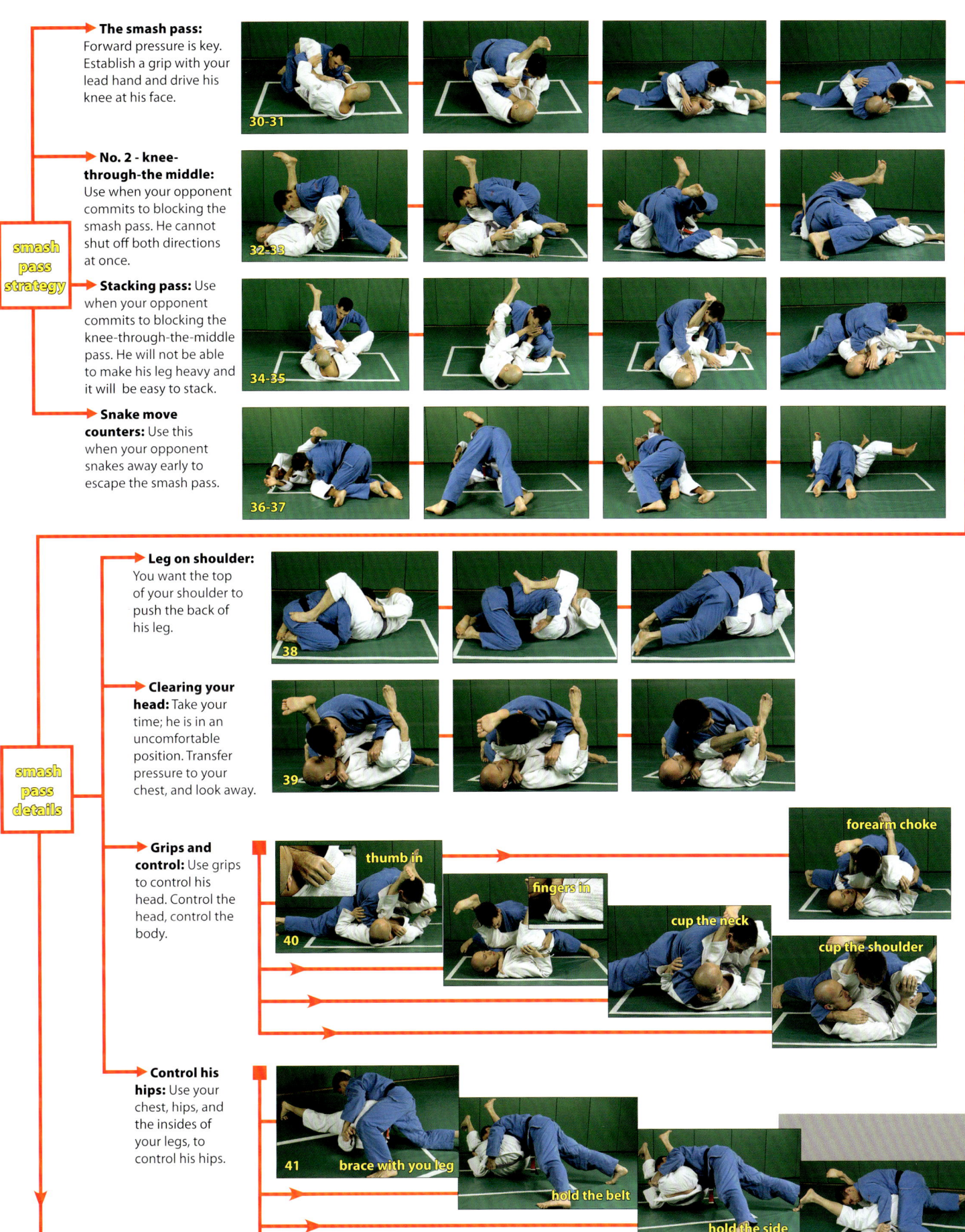

defeating smash pass counters

- **Knee from the outside:** Collapse his elbow from the outside with your knee.

- **Knee from the inside:** Collapse his elbow from the inside with your knee.

- **Wrist jam:** Use when his hands block your hips and his wrists are already cocked back a little.

- **Switch sides:** Use when his knees are close and he commits to blocking one side.

- **Knee on belly:** Use when he is able to bring his knee in front of you to block the smash pass. Wedge your knee in the space between his thigh and his stomach.

- **Turtle prevention:** Stop your opponent from going to his hands and knees by pinning the arm on the side you are passing to with your foot.

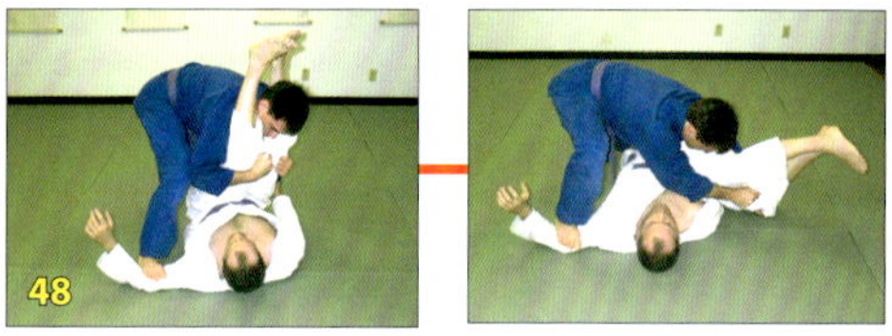

- **Turtle prevention:** You can also stop your opponent by putting your knee over his arm.

The details to finishing the smash pass apply to many guard passes.

attacks from the smash pass

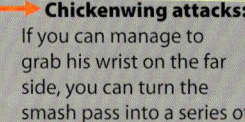

- **Chickenwing attacks:** If you can manage to grab his wrist on the far side, you can turn the smash pass into a series of submissions.

combat base passes

- **Knee-in-the-middle pass:** This pass is a good option anytime you can get your arm under one of his legs.

- **Reverse knee-in-the-middle pass:** You can drive either knee through to pass, or pass to either side. You go must not let him get an under-hook if you go this way.

- **vs. under-hook:** If he do get an under-hook, this might work. Reach back and hold his belt. Use the side of your head to push his head as you pass.

- **Margarida grip:** Use this grip if you cannot get the under-hook.

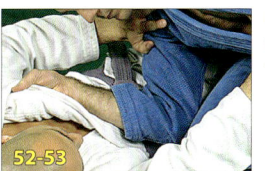

Freeing your trapped foot: Use one foot to free the other.

double under-hooks

- **Double under-hooks:** In this variation, you pop up into their hips, controlling his hips between yours on the way to passing.

   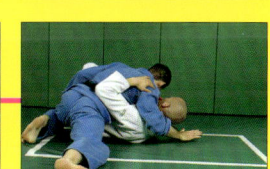

- **Double under-hooks (ramp):** Hold his belt with both hands as you pull him on top of your thighs on the way to passing.

- **Clearing hooks:** Clear butterfly hooks by donkey-kicking one leg then the other. Move in tight so it does not happen again.

alternate smash series

- **Entry while trapping the off leg:** Trap one leg between your side, triceps, and thigh. Use the other arm to under-hook.

- **Getting the under-hook:** Hold your own shin, then use that same leg for power to lift his leg.

- **Snake move counter:** As he turn to his side, drop your body on the inside of his knee and then clear it.

⟳ There are many opportunities to pass if you can drop down on the outside of your opponent's leg.

scissor guard passes

▶ **Knee-in-chest counter:** Push from the outside as you force his knee across your body. Drop your weight down, then clear his legs.

▶ **Clear the top leg:** Cup his top leg with your hand and pull, bringing it back and yourself around. Slide your back knee to his hips.

▶ **Beating stiff arms:** If he posts his arms into your chest, drive forward and to the knee-in-belly position.

▶ **Clear the bottom leg:** If, when you clear the top leg, he tries to bring in his bottom leg, jump over it as it comes.

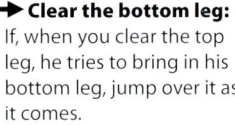

▶ **Trap the top leg:** If he posts his arms in your chest and puts his top leg in front of his bottom leg, pin his top knee with your instep and step over his legs into the mount.

▶ **Trap the top leg:** Just like above, only instead of moving to the mount, you circle behind him and then go to side control.

▶ **Trap the top leg:** If your upper body is close to his, you can use your other leg to trap his top leg. If he turns back his hips, you are pulled into the mount.

▶ **Trap the top leg:** If he does not turn back his hips, hook over your instep and then proceed as with the first two trap-the-top-leg techniques.

▶ **Flip over:** Consider this when his top knee/leg blocks your hip but you are at a right angle to his torso.

▶ **Ankle trap:** Scoop your arm in front of his instep, then grip his belt. Keep his top knee down with your chest as you pass.

🌀 *By dropping your shoulder into your opponent's hips you interfere with his ability to move, allowing you to pass.*

shoulder on hips passes

- **Low mount:** Scoop both his legs into your leg triangle, then flatten out his legs. Work your way up an inch at a time.

- **Simple hopping pass:** Plant your shoulder in his belly. Hold one knee and look the other way. Jump as you push down on the knee.

- **Springing shoulder pass:** Momentarily stick his feet to the mat by holding at the insides of his knees. The foot opposite the way you are jumping goes first.

- **Leg trap pass 1:** Switch your hips to get then around his knee. Base on your shoulder and opposite foot as you switch your hips back to facing the mat.

- **Leg trap pass 2:** You can control his leg by trapping it with your forearm.

- **Leg trap pass 3:** You can control his leg with your other arm by wrapping it up and using a monkey grip on his shin.

- **One leg at a time:** You will not always clear both hooks by jumping. Clear one hook at a time if need be.

- **Bridging pass:** Drop all your weight into his belly as you flip. Make sure not to roll past his head as you turn back over. Your butt never touches the mat.

- **Somersault pass:** Land with both feet to one side and do not roll past his head as you turn back over. Your butt never touches the mat.

- **Spin pass:** Use this when both his hands are on your torso. Be bold, but don't roll past his head.

sitting guard passes

- **Sitting guard:** Your opponent wants his head against your chest and an under-hook. You position yourself to deny him both.

☯ Use your opponent's sitting posture to your advantage, knock him down over his under-hooking shoulder.

- **Body lock pass:** Push his knee across his body and drop your weight on it. Replace the pushing hand with the instep of your opposite foot. Climb over his top leg.

- **Mount:** You can also transition to the mount from the body lock pass. This way is more simple but provides less control of the opponent's legs.

- **Sitting guard passes:** In each of the three techniques, you pass to the side of the under-hook by dropping down on it and lifting his legs.

ankle pick

lasso grip

whizzer

☯ Use these techniques to finish your guard passes and to prevent your opponent's escape.

escape prevention

- **He rolls away:** You can prevent your opponent from getting to his hands and knees by blocking his neck with a choke, controlling the top arm, controlling the bottom hand, or controlling the head and arms.

forearm choke

figure-four

bottom arm

top arm

head and arm

- **Diagonal grip:** As he turns to the turtle position, shoot your leg between his and take an over-under grip over the opposite shoulder from the rear.

diagonal grip

- **He rolls into you:** Use a cross-face grip to block his head.

cross-face
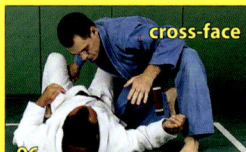 

Chapter 3

Standing Guard Passes

Besides breaking and passing the guard on the knees, the other option is to stand and pass. As with passing on the knees, there are relative advantages and disadvantages to the standing passes. In general, passing the guard while standing allows the fighter to use the advantage of speed over strength. Very often the smaller and lighter fighter will find it easier to pass the guard standing. It is sometimes easier to break a very tight closed guard by standing first. Standing results in the opponent's hips being lifted off the mat, negating much of the power and mobility he has with his hips down. With the opponent hanging from your hips in the closed guard as you stand, gravity is on your side as your opponent must use considerable energy just to hang on with his legs. Very often, pressing down on the inside of the opponent's knees or wedging a knee in between his legs will be sufficient to break the guard. The downside of standing to break a closed guard is that you are left more vulnerable to sweeps, as your center of gravity is higher and your base is smaller than it is when you are on your knees.

Although standing to pass the guard allows you to use speed to your advantage, it also generally requires more energy expenditure than passes from the knees. The advantage to the freedom of movement standing affords is the potential to build up considerable momentum. You can build momentum in your own movements (side to side, for example) and pass with speed, or you can build up momentum to move or control the opponent's legs as you pass. When standing, the possibility of jumping or cart wheeling passes also arises.

Most of the submissions available from the guard are also available when you are standing. Your vulnerability to sweeps is, however, typically higher when standing to pass. When standing, your center of gravity is higher and your base smaller. The opponent basically has two categories of sweep available. First, the opponent grabs or blocks your ankles or feet, attempting to trip you backward. Second, the opponent has control of your arms or upper body and his foot or feet in your hips. Here, there is the possibility of being swept sideways or head first in a roll.

As you pass the guard, it is important to pay constant attention to the positioning of your opponent's hands, feet, and hips, so that you can adjust your position and reduce or eliminate the potential to be swept. While standing, you are also vulnerable to the opponent's spider guard (his feet in your biceps as he pulls on your sleeves) or De La Riva position (the opponent's leg wrapped around the outside of your leg and inserted between your legs from the rear) and the X-guard (the opponent crosses his shins like an X, and controls one of your legs with his insteps while holding your other leg with his arm.

Other possible dangers while standing are foot locks, knee bars, and heel hooks. All are more easily set up by your opponent when you are standing. You must be on guard against leg submissions if the opponent threads his leg around yours from between your legs, or if he begins to turn and trap your leg between his legs. Foot locks are also set up if the opponent trips you backward onto the mat. On the other hand, you too have many opportunities to attack the opponent's legs as you pass the guard standing. These techniques are covered later in **Chapters 4 & 5**. One final category of attack to guard against is the potential for the opponent quickly to go to his knees and shoot for a single or double leg takedown.

Standing Up

Blue fixes his grips in the guard. He gathers the cloth near White's armpits.

Holding White's hips down, Blue shifts his weight to his right and lifts his left knee, posting his left foot on the mat.

Blue brings his weight back to center.

> Before you can pass the guard standing up, you need to be standing up. Here are a few methods for getting to your feet.

Blue fixes his grips in White's guard.

Blue pushes down on White and postures.

Blue hops up onto both feet simultaneously.

You can pop off your toes (see the can opener to the right) or from your insteps (below).

STANDING AND OPENING

Blue lifts his right knee and comes to the squat position.

Blue stands up.

Holding White down with his right arm, Blue pushes down on the inside of White's right knee to break open the guard.

Blue drops his hips a little and pinches inward with his knees.

> This one works best without the gi.

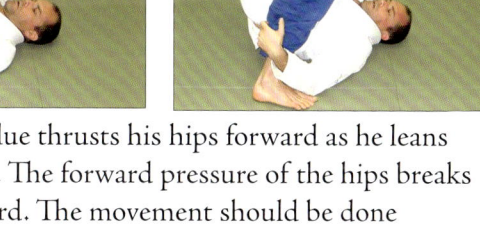
After standing, Blue thrusts his hips forward as he leans backward slightly. The forward pressure of the hips breaks open White's guard. The movement should be done explosively

STANDING CAN OPENER

Blue holds the back of White's head with both hands. (He holds the back of the head, not behind the neck.) Blue pinches the outsides of White's hips with his knees as he pulls White's head forward and downward, trying to force White's chin to his chest. At the same time, Blue squats and pushes forward with his hips. The pressure on the back of White's neck causes him to open his feet.

Elbow opener

The techniques on this page look alike. We are, however, trying to show two different things: Using the elbow to break open the guard and using the knee in the middle to break open the guard. As a practical matter, you will often combine the two, which is what is going on in the pictures.

Blue stands in White's guard.

Holding White down with his right hand, Blue holds the cloth inside White's left thigh and presses his elbow inside White's right knee.

Blue steps back with his left foot.

Knee-in opener

This technique is very effective and is a go-to move for opening the guard. It puts mechanical advantage and gravity to work for you. By squaring up your knee to your opponent's tailbone and then putting your back into his legs, you make him very uncomfortable. This one is referred to as **the violator** for obvious reasons. Here, Blue is using the elbow opener technique from above for added effect. Keeping an elbow to the inside makes it easier to swim that arm under his leg, which makes for an easy transition to an under-hook when his legs do open. An elbow in is not necessary, however; you can also perform this technique with your elbows to the outside of his legs, in which case you would push on the front edge of his hip with the palm of your hand.

Blue positions his hands to use them as base as he stands.

Note how Blue's head moves over White's head as Blue stands. Lunging forward as you come up makes it much easier to get your hips up with your opponent hanging on.

Once your hips are up, hop forward.

Standing and Opening

Blue pushes down with his left elbow, dropping his weight into it; and breaks open White's guard.

Blue inserts his right knee between White's legs as he lowers his hips.

Blue drives his left knee through the middle and begins to pass the guard.

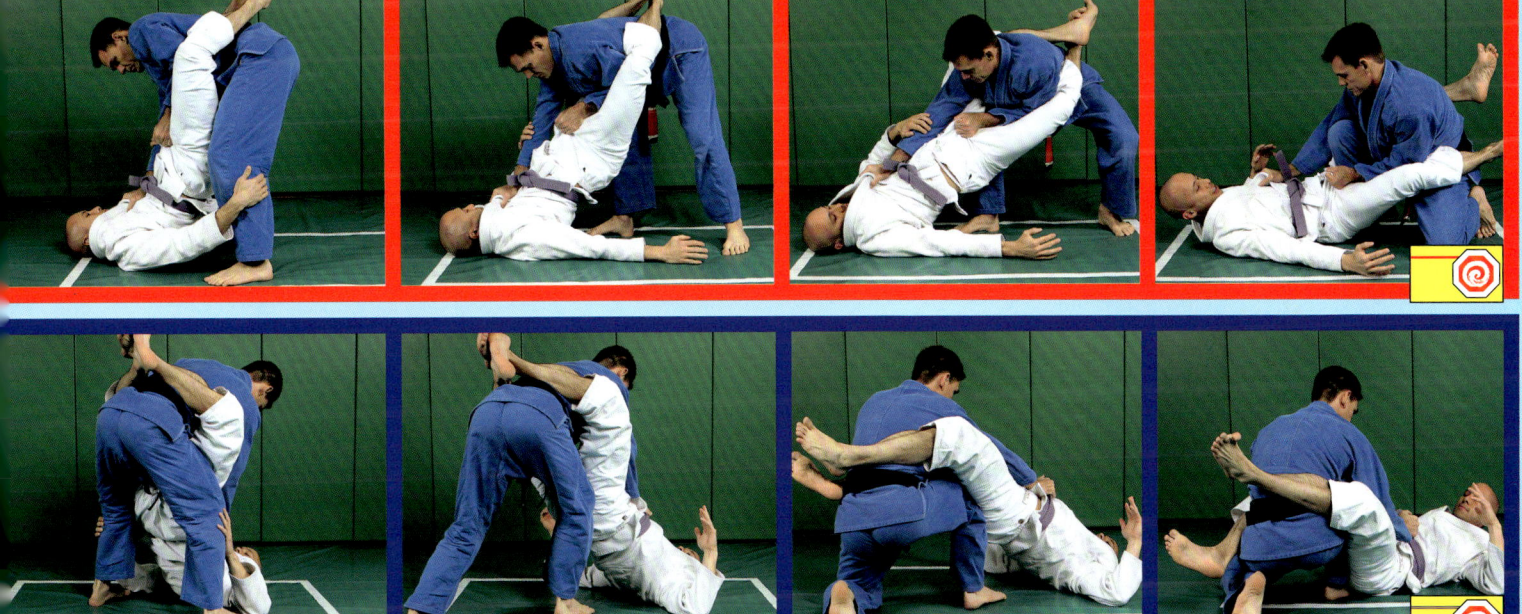

Blue stands and adjusts his grips. His right hand holds a lapel for defense and stability. His right elbow moves inside White's leg.

Blue positions his right knee right in front of White's tailbone, then steps back with his left foot.

Blue bends at the knees, thrusting his right knee forward as he moves his lower back the opposite direction.

The pressure into White's tailbone and from Blue's back is more than White can withstand; his guard opens.

108 STANDING PASSES ❖ STANDING AND OPENING

IF THE KNEE-IN-THE-MIDDLE DOES NOT OPEN THE GUARD...

Sometimes the knee-in-the-middle technique fails to open the guard. Usually it is because the guard player has long legs or you have short ones. Whatever the case, you can pass through his closed guard by continuing to drive your knee through to either side of his torso. Here we show a cross-knee guard pass.

Blue stands in White's guard.

Blue puts his right knee in the center of White's rear and steps back with his left foot.

🌀 All the variations to the cross-knee guard pass from pgs. 50-53 work here. You could also drive your knee to the other side of your opponent's body, similar to the technique on pg. 49.

Once Blue has his right knee up between White's legs, he is ready to complete the pass.

Blue drives his right knee across the top of White's right hip. The change in the angles of pressure opens White's guard.

Pushing down on White's hips, Blue lowers his hips.

Blue drives his right knee up between White's legs.

As Blue lowers his hips to the full squatting position, his knee is up between White's legs.

Continuing the forward pressure of his hips, Blue lowers his upper body and under-hooks White's left arm with his right arm. Blue cross-faces White.

Keeping pressure down on White's upper body, Blue steps over his right leg with his left foot.

Blue turns right, brings his left knee up close to White's right shoulder, and completes the pass.

110 STANDING PASSES ❖ STANDING AND OPENING

CROSS-GRIP OPENER

By establishing a cross-grip on your opponent's sleeve and standing, you nullify most of his primary sweep options. You can take the grip before or after you stand, though it is easier to get it before. Having prevented the sweeps, your other arm is free to make pressure on his knee to open his closed guard.

Blue fixes his grips in White's guard.

Blue grabs White's right sleeve with his right hand.

Blue pulls White's right arm across to Blue's right side, grabs White's lapel with his left hand pressing down on top of White's right forearm, and posts his left foot on the mat. Blue steps up with his left foot first because White is unable to grab Blue's left foot with his controlled right hand.

Blue posts his right foot on the mat and stands.

Blue pulls up on White's right arm and presses down on the inside of White's right knee to break the guard.

Blue squats and pushes with his left knee against White's right knee forcing it to the mat. Blue's left arm pushes rights knee down.

Blue lowers his body, slides his left knee over the inside of White's right upper thigh, and starts the near knee pass.

112 STANDING PASSES ❖ STACKING PASS

STACKING PASS FROM STANDING CROSS GRIP

Here, again, the cross grip is put to use. The loop created by the legs in the closed guard is resilient against pressure from most directions, but not all. This technique exploits a weak angle. It is hard for the guard player to stop his top foot from being lifted up and away from his lower foot, which is how this one works. Note that you must do this so that you are lifting against the top foot; trying to lift the bottom one will get your arm stuck in an awkward position.

Blue controls White's right arm with the cross grip and stands.

Blue reaches back with his left hand and inserts his hand between his left hip and White's crossed ankles.

Blue lifts White's leg until the guard opens. As soon as it does, Blue immediately lowers his hips a little and slides his left arm through.

STACKING PASS

Blue hooks his left elbow around White's left calf, Blue twists his hips to his left to break White's guard.

Blue lowers his weight onto White and grabs inside White's left collar with a right thumb-in grip.

Blue sprawls his hips back and smashes his weight into White.

CRUSH-CHOKE GUARD OPENERS

Crush chokes against the guard usually don't result in submissions, but they are good for opening the guard. Be ready for armbar attempts against you if your opponent holds one of your arms with both of his.

Blue stands in White's closed guard and grabs his lapels with four fingers in on each side.

Blue pushes his right fist across White's throat. Blue pulls the cloth over his right fist with his left hand.

Blue leans his weight forward into White, pushing down across White's throat with his right hand. The pressure causes White to react by opening his guard so that he can move away to defend the choke.

In this variation, Blue stands in White's closed guard and grabs inside the lapels, fingers in and thumbs up. There must not be any slack in the gi.

Blue pushes both fists into the sides of White's neck by rolling his big knuckles in. His knuckles go from pointing at each other to pointing at the ground.

Ankle Sweep & Counter

Attack

You need to stay ready when standing in the closed guard. The instant your opponent opens his legs, you should expect an attack.

> When you are standing and have opened the guard, you must beware of ankle sweeps.

White stands in Blue's guard to begin his pass.

Blue grabs behind both of White's ankles, as close to White's heels as possible.

Blue slides his hips forward underneath White. He pinches his knees together.

Holding White's feet, Blue pushes with his legs to sweep White onto his butt. Blue keeps his hips on the mat during the push. As White begins to fall, Blue sits up.

Blue quickly grabs White's lapel with his left hand so that he can pull himself up to the mount.

Blue bends his left leg back and pulls himself up to the mount.

Defense

Simple counters are often the best. By grabbing your opponent's gi, you can counter a lot of sweeps.

As White attempts to sweep Blue, Blue grabs both of White's lapels and pulls himself down to counter the backwards push of the sweep.

116 STANDING PASSES ❖ STANDING AND OPENING

KNEE SMASH TO SMASH PASS

Here is an option for if you are standing but your opponent's back is on the ground and his guard is closed. Proceed cautiously and look out for sweeps and the *omo plata*.

Blue stands in White's guard.

Blue brings his left elbow inside White's right knee and pushes down on White's hips with his right arm as he begins to twist his hips to his right. Blue's right knee makes pressure sideways into White's hip.

Blue continues twisting his hips to his right as he drives his right knee across White's ribs. The torque and pressure break open White's guard.

SMASH PASS FOLLOW-UP

This technique works very well in combination with the one above. This is the same combination we showed for use with the smash-pass in **Ch. 2**. It is worth repeating because they work very well together and we want to drive home that point. Start with the smash pass, then alternate to this one if need be. Threaten with one to open up the other.

Blue attempts the under-hook smash pass. White stops the pass by stiff-arming Blue's right hip.

Blue changes directions and pushes down on White's right knee, then brings his left knee between White's legs.

Driving his weight forward, White slides his left knee over the top of White's right leg, as close to White's hip as possible.

Lowering his upper body, Blue under-hooks White's head with his left arm.

THE FAST VERSION

To the right is a sequence demonstrating the fast and loose version of the pass shown above. Notice in this faster version that Blue never turns his hips away from the mat. This is an easier movement, but it needs to be done quickly, in one quick hop. An effective ploy is to switch from a methodical pass to one relying on quickness without warning.

STANDING AND OPENING

Keeping his weight down, Blue releases his right grip.

Blue under-hooks White's left leg and begins to lower his body.

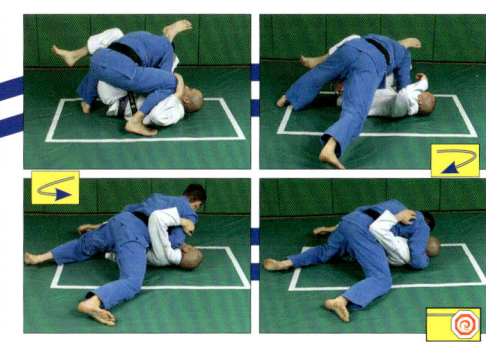

After securing the collar with a thumb-in grip, Blue proceeds with the basic smash pass from **Ch. 2**. Blue sprawls his hips back, smashes White, twists his hips to his right, and completes the pass.

Keeping his left foot hooked over the top of White's right thigh, Blue begins to step his right leg back out of the guard.

Blue drops his left hip to the mat and posts his right foot without dropping his hips. During the movement, Blue keeps driving his weight into White.

Blue scissors his left leg under his right toward White's head.

Blue establishes the side control position.

118 STANDING PASSES ❖ STANDING AND OPENING

OPENING THE CLOSED GUARD OF A HANGING OPPONENT

Sometimes your opponent may jump into the guard while you are standing. Other times you might lift him up from off his back. Either way, you are carrying his weight. Start with a wide base to make holding him up easier while you establish your balance and grips. Do not let him hug his chest to yours. If he tries block them with your arms. It is work holding him up, but it takes energy on his part also. Use gravity to your advantage by pushing down his legs as he hangs from you.

Starting with a wide base, Blue stands in White's guard.

White hangs on to Blue's lapel and pulls himself up off the mat to preserve his closed guard and attack.

Blue puts his right palm on the inside of White's left knee.

Blue pushes White's left leg down to the mat, breaking White's guard.

IF HE DOESN'T OPEN HIS GUARD...

Some players are tenacious when it comes to keeping their feet crossed. You sometimes just have to accept that you are not going to be able to open their legs and that you must find another way. This is an alternative to the move above for just such a situation.

Blue stands in White's guard. White hangs on and pulls himself up.

Blue pushes down on the inside of White's left knee.

Blue brings his feet closer together so that there is less for White to sit on. Blue breaks open White's guard and pushes White's hips to the mat.

Blue lowers his hips and begins turning them to his right.

STANDING AND OPENING

Blue lowers his hips and drops his right knee over the top of White's left thigh, close to his hip.

Blue lowers his upper body and under-hooks White's head with his right arm. It is important for Blue to keep his right foot hooked over the top of White's left thigh, preventing White from trapping Blue's right leg in the half guard.

Blue drops his right hip to the mat as he whips his left leg back to his left. Blue posts his left foot at a 90-degree angle to White's body. Blue maintains his control over White's right leg.

Blue scissors his right leg back under his left leg and brings his left knee in to block White's hip.

> Remember not to let your opponent get the under-hook, or there is a risk that he could take your back at the end of the pass.

Blue continues his movement and begins to slide his left knee over the top of White's left upper thigh. Blue also grabs White's left arm with his right hand.

Blue drives his hips through, pushing his knees to the mat as he simultaneously pulls back on White's left arm.

Blue continues pulling up on White's left arm and lays his weight on White's chest as he drives his hips over White's left hip.

Blue scissors his left leg ahead and comes into the modified scarf hold position.

OPENING THE CLOSED GUARD OF A HANGING OPPONENT 2

This is another good option for dealing with a hard to break open closed guard. By lifting your opponent's top foot off his bottom foot, you open up his legs in a direction from which they cannot put up much resistance; the body is just not strong this way, particularly when your opponent is already hanging off your body. Once you have his legs open and get your collar grip, this is a smash pass variation.

Blue stands in White's guard. White hangs on and pulls himself up. In the top row, White helps keep himself up by bracing his left hand on Blue's right knee.

Blue reaches back with his left hand. Blue is careful to pick the one of White's legs that is on top of the other.

Blue inserts his right hand between his hips and White's ankles.

Blue slides his right arm in and hooks under White's left ankle. Blue pushes White down with his left hand and breaks the guard.

CAGING THE HIPS FROM STANDING

If your opponent does open his legs while hanging from your standing position, you need to take advantage of it quickly before he can fix his guard. In this technique, you do so by using your legs and your weight to immobilize his hips and legs as you under-hook either of his legs.

Blue pushes downward on White's hips with both hands. Blue makes pressure in one direction with his arms and the other way with his back.

Blue bends over and pushes White onto the mat, breaking open his guard.

Standing and Opening

Blue pushes White to the mat.

Blue lowers his hips and drives his weight forward onto White. Blue grabs inside White's right collar with his right hand, thumb in, and smashes White's left knee into his face.

Blue bases his legs wide and smashes his weight forward into White.

Blue drops his right side, lifts his head, and clears White's left leg, moving into the side control position.

To maintain control of White's hips and prevent him from fixing his feet, Blue moves forward and pinches his knees together, trapping White's knees together.

Blue lifts his upper body and clears his arms. Blue maintains his forward pressure and then squeezes with his knees, sitting on the back of White's legs.

Blue's right hand pushes White's left ankle across Blue's torso. Blue lowers his level and turns his hips to his left. Blue under-hooks White's head with his right arm.

Blue sprawls his legs back and drives his weight forward, passing the guard.

Over and back

Here is an unorthodox but effective way of passing the guard. Like the last technique, this technique is premised on sitting on the back of your opponent's legs as you pinch in your knees in order to control his hips. There are a number of ways that you could arrive at the position, one of which is shown on the previous spread. You might also get here against a player who use a collapse-and-fold style of guard. The technique probably is best against players your own size or smaller. It definitely is a good one for heavy guys to use against quicker, smaller ones.

You cannot do this move halfway; it's all or nothing. Don't worry too much about crashing down on your opponent; there isn't really any crashing involved because your hips are connected your entire way down.

◀▶ In the open guard, Blue pushes White's legs up and pushes his pelvis forward, moving up to sit over the backs of White's legs.

◀▶ Blue sits all his weight on top of White, and by bringing his knees slightly together, pinches White's legs into one another. This helps to control White's hips momentarily.

◀▶ Blue swings his right foot across White's hips and all the way across his body until Blue's foot is outside White's right hip.

The way you control the opponent's hips at the beginning is the same as in the previous technique.

◀▶ Blue turns his hips and uses his weight to press White's legs to the mat. Blue simultaneously lays his body on top of White's torso. Blue maintains constant pressure on top of his opponent as he does the move. The contact point of the pressure begins with the inside of the upper thigh, then moves to his butt, then to his hip.

◀▶ Just before Blue's right foot touches the mat, he twists his body back to the right, swinging his left foot over White's legs, and lands on his knees in side control. Blue scoops his left arm under White's head so that White cannot turn to his hands and knees.

Over and Back

◉ Do not attempt this move if your opponent has grabbed both of your ankles; you will get swept.

◉ The foot that swings over should not touch the mat until your hips are all the way down.

If there is space to thread your arm in, take the under-hook.

Cross-face your opponent if you cannot under-hook his top arm.

124 STANDING PASSES ❖ FREEING THE ARMS

GETTING OUT OF THE SPIDER GUARD

It is a simple matter to go back and forth from your knees to your feet when you are in the spider guard, so they are treated together here. When you are confronted with the spider guard, you need to get your opponent's feet off your biceps before you attempt to pass or in coordination with your pass. Over the next six pages, we go over options for freeing the arms in order to pass.

White is holding Blue in the spider guard by controlling Blue's right sleeve and upper arm. White pulls with his left hand and pushes with his left foot to control Blue's right arm.

Blue steps his right foot onto the mat and brings his hips forward.

Blue suddenly jerks his right arm downward, causing White's left ankle to hit the top of Blue's right knee. White's left foot is caught on top of Blue's knee, and Blue continues to pull his right arm down, knocking White's foot off his upper arm.

Blue now under-hooks White's left leg with his right arm and reaches for White's right collar. From here, Blue will smash and then pass White's guard.

Freeing the Arms

125

◀▶ White has his left foot on Blue's biceps. White grips the cloth inside White's ankle.

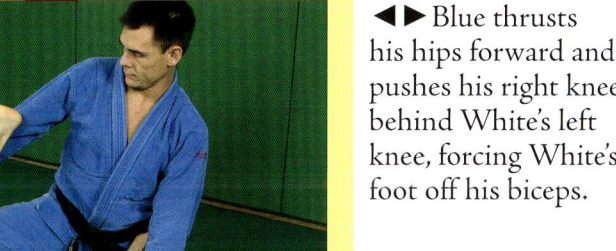

◀▶ Blue brings his left knee up inside White's left leg.

◀▶ Blue thrusts his hips forward and pushes his right knee behind White's left knee, forcing White's foot off his biceps.

◀ Blue pushes White's left leg across to White's right side.

▶ Alternatively, Blue can use his hand to control White's leg after getting it off his elbow. Blue won't be able to control White's leg for long this way, but long enough.

◀▶ Continuing the motion, Blue passes the guard. From here he might use one of the techniques from pages 94-96 to keep White from rolling away.

126 STANDING PASSES ❖ FREEING THE ARMS

REMOVING FEET/ CONTROLLING LEGS

Here we see two techniques in one for clearing the arms. You might find your arms in this position when you are on your knees and then stand to free them, or this could happen while you are standing. Either way, clearing the grips is the first priority.

Blue is caught in White's spider guard. White holds Blue's sleeves and pushes his feet into Blue's biceps.

Blue squats and puts his right knee into the back of White's left calf. Blue pushes forward with his right knee, clearing his right arm.

Blue lowers his level and underhooks White's left leg with his right arm.

Blue turns to his right and moves his left leg forward.

Blue twists to his right and pushes with his left knee against the back of White's knee, taking White's right foot off his left biceps.

Blue pushes White's right leg across to his left and lowers his body into the side control position.

Freeing the Arms

Removing feet: hand techniques

Blue stands in White's guard. White has trapped Blue in the spider guard. (see previous page)

Blue brings his forearms behind White's calves.

Blue moves forward and simultaneously pushes White's legs away from him. The pressure clears White's feet off Blue's upper arms.

▶ Blue grabs inside White's ankles and sits on the back of White's legs to control his movement, or ▶ inside White's knees. Blue simultaneously lowers his hips and pinches in with his knees.

▶ Blue changes his left grip to the outside of White's right ankle, ▶ or he puts his forearm into the side of White's knee and pushes White's right leg to White's left as he moves around White's right side.

Standing Passes ❖ Freeing the Arms

REMOVING FEET WITH FEET
Your legs are free when you are in the spider guard, so use them.

Blue is caught in White's spider guard.

Blue holds outside White's knees and places his left foot on the inside of White's right knee.

Blue uses his weight to push White's right leg to the mat.

Blue now twists his body to his left and, using his torso, pushes White's left leg across to White's right. Blue is now clear to pass to White's left side.

REMOVING FEET WITH ELBOWS (FROM THE HIP)...

Blue stands in White's open guard. White holds Blue's left sleeve with his right hand and pushes his right foot into White's left upper arm. White pushes his left foot into White's right hip.

Blue holds inside White's left knee with his right hand. Blue slides his right foot back a little and lowers his left elbow under White's left knee.

Blue pushes up his left elbow, levering White's left foot off his hip.

... AND KNEES (FROM SPIDER GUARD)

Blue puts his left knee behind White's right knee.

Blue pushes behind White's right knee with his left knee and forces White's right foot off his arm.

Blue lowers his body and underhooks White's head with his left arm. Blue has now set up the near-knee-pass.

FREEING THE ARMS

DUCK PASS

Practice this slowly until you can do it smoothly without putting much pressure on your neck. Execute it boldly.

Blue is in White's spider guard, but White only has control of one of Blue's arms.

Blue reaches across with his left hand and grabs over the top of White's left thigh. Blue will pull with his left arm to make ducking his head around White's knee easier.

Blue ducks his head around White's knee so that the bottom of his neck/top of his shoulders push against White's leg. Blue looks upward as he pulls White's left leg to his left with his left hand. Blue simultaneously steps his left leg across to his right and ducks his head under White's leg.

Blue pivots around his left foot and swings his right leg around.

▲This column illustrates Blue's body movement during the pass.

◉ Blue makes a wide base.

◉ Keeping his back straight, Blue lowers his head.

◉ Blue steps through with his left foot, lifts his head, and looks upward as he thrusts his hips forward.

◉ Make sure as you step through that you keep pressure on the opponent's leg with the base of your neck.

Blue establishes side control, using the grip on White's leg to control White from escaping.

130 STANDING PASSES ◆ FEET ON THE HIPS

FEET ON THE HIPS:

The portion of this chapter deals with the situation where your opponent's feet are on your hips. Freeing your arms from your opponent's grips is not as important here as it was with the spider guard. In fact, for some of the passes we show, it is not necessary at all. The greater danger when your opponent's feet are on your hips is that he can use the power of his legs to move your hips to his advantage. Be especially careful if he gets control of either of your legs with his arms.

ELBOW UNDER-HOOK SMASH PASS

Getting good grips on the inside of your opponent's knees allows you to use your forearms to control the back of his legs. Use your grips as leverage points for your forearms.

Blue is standing in White's open guard, holding the cloth inside White's knees, thumbs in.

Blue lowers his level, circling his right elbow under White's left knee (maintain the grip on the inside of the knee). Once his elbow is under, Blue pops White's left foot off of his hip.

◉ Use the power of your legs and body to push the opponent's leg across, not just the upper body.

Blue pushes off with his right foot, twisting his body to his left and pushing White's left knee across his body, and passes around White's left side.

Here is a different view of the grips and position of the elbow.

The finish of the guard pass is a matter of forward pressure. Be wary of an opponent's attempts to go to his knees.
More on preventing that next.

JUMP AWAY:

By hopping backward while pushing down on the inside of your opponent's knees you can make space between the soles of his feet and your body. Once that happens, you will have a chance to force his feet to the mat and move to his side.

Blue stands in White's guard. White has his feet in Blue's hips. Blue grabs inside White's knees with both hands.

Blue hops his feet back and pushes down on White's knees, clearing White's feet off his hips and forcing White's feet to the mat.

Blue begins to move to his right as he simultaneously pushes White's legs to his left.

Blue lowers his right shoulder onto White's left hip as he continues to push White's knees away from him.

Blue drops his weight on White's hips and passes the guard.

Leapfrog Pass

Blue stands in White's open guard. Blue holds the cloth inside White's knees.

Blue hops back, bends forward and pushes White's feet to the mat with his body weight.

Blue pushes down White's knees and leapfrogs over White's knees. Blue continues to push White's knees until he clears them.

Blue thrusts his hips forward and drops to his knees in top mount.

As Blue attempts the *leapfrog pass*, White defends by pushing up behind Blue's legs in an attempt to throw Blue over his head.

Blue counters by leaning to one side and scissoring his legs. The momentum carries him through a 3/4 turn and into side control.

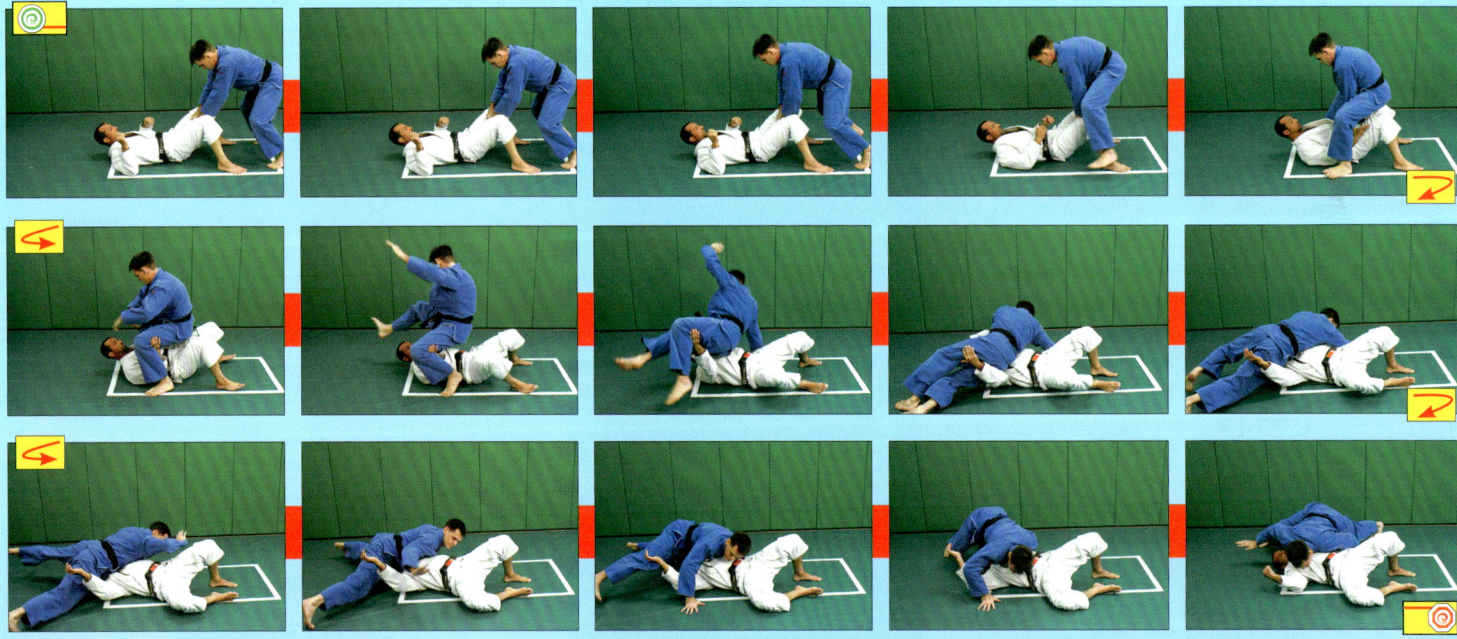

Butterfly Hooks

Over the Top

Sometimes a player focuses so much of his effort on preventing you from coming around or under his legs that he does not defend against your coming over the top. This technique works well against opponents with shorter legs. Elements of boldness and surprise are key.

◀▶ Blue is standing in White's open guard. White has his feet hooked inside Blue's knees. Blue holds the insides of White's knees and uses his weight to push White's right leg to the mat.

◀▶ Blue moves his right elbow up and begins to push down on White's left leg. He wants to drive White's foot to the mat while using the driving hand to help lift his hips over White's knee.

◀▶ Blue shoves White's left leg between his legs and turns his hips as he begins to lower his weight.

This one often results in a half-guard situation. Passing the half-guard is examined in the next chapter.

◀▶ Blue drops his weight and his left knee over White's right leg to top mount.

134 STANDING PASSES ❖ FEET ON THE HIPS

KNEE AGAINST KNEE

The key to this technique is pinning your opponent's top knee in front of his bottom knee and then establishing some sort of grip on his upper body to prevent him from going to his knees.

Use the top part of your shin or your knee against the crease behind his knee and then put your weight into it. With the top knee pinned in front of the bottom, he cannot turn to his back.

As the sequence begins, White's feet are in Blue's hips. The technique could begin with White's feet in a variety of other positions as well. The important thing is that you smash the top knee in front of, or even on top of, the bottom knee.

Blue pushes his left hand against the side of White's left shin. Blue begins moving his left leg in behind White' right knee.

Blue angles his left foot in so that the top of his shin can fit in behind White's left knee.

The combined force of Blue's left hand and foot, along with the element of surprise, turn White on his left side. Blue drops his weight into White's knee. He wants to drive the knee forward and across.

Feet on the Hips

Blue has forced White's top knee above and in front of his bottom knee. Blue swims in an underhook with his left arm so that White cannot go to the turtle position. Alternatively, Blue could have also used his right arm to hold White's left arm or lapel to keep him from going to his knees.

Continuing to make White's right knee carry most of his weight, Blue lowers his upper body down on White, controlling White's right sleeve as he goes.

Blue adjusts his right foot forward, shifts some weight chest-to-chest against White, slides his left leg off White's knee, and then brings it under his left leg.

Blue continues to pull up on White's arm as he sits through for the finish.

136 Standing Passes ❖ Butterfly Hooks

Knee against knee 2

This is another variation on the knee against knee pass from the previous spread. In the photos, White is not doing anything with his arms. Suppose, however, that after Blue pinned one of White's knees in front of the other, that White were to straight-arm Blue's torso so that he could not continue forward as in the last spread. The solution would be for Blue to go to White's backside and obtain side control from there, which is what Blue does here.

Blue grabs White's chest lapels with both hands.

Pushing down with his weight on White's chest, Blue leans forward and begins to lift his hips.

Blue hops up and lands with his feet parallel, outside White's hips.

Blue pushes White's left leg across and down with his left hand while maintaining control on White's lapel with his right hand. Blue keeps his left arm straight so that he can transfer the weight of his upper body through his arm.

Blue slides his left shin across the top of White's right thigh, pinning White's legs together with his weight (Blue leans his weight to his left, over White's legs).

Blue lays his weight on top of White and reaches his left arm around the back of White's head.

Butterfly Hooks

Another difference between this version of the pass and the last is that here Blue uses his left hand to shove White's right knee across his body before he goes knee against knee. In the previous technique, Blue used his knee to push White's knee from the onset. Either way is good; experiment with both.

Blue grabs outside White's right knee with his left hand.

Blue drives his weight to his right and begins to push White's right knee down to White's left.

Blue continues to push White's right knee down on top of his left knee.

Blue twists up to his right and kicks his right leg back over to his rear. Blue holds White's knee with his right hand as in the photos for added control, but he could finish the pass without that grip also.

Hopping over White's right hip, Blue scissors his left leg back below his right.

Blue lands in side control at White's right side.

Leg drag

This technique works even when the opponent has a firm grip on both your sleeves. In other words, it can be done without first breaking his grip. Your opponent has to crunch forward to keep his grips, which causes his back to curve, which makes it easier to spin him on his back.

White has his feet on Blue's hips and a grip on Blue's sleeves.

Blue lowers his base, grabs White's right sleeve, and reaches around the outside of White's leg with his right arm.

Blue grabs cloth near White's knee. At the same time, Blue grabs White's right sleeve with his left hand.

Blue steps back with his left foot to help clear White's leg from Blue's left hip. As soon as he has made a little space, he begins pulling White's legs to the side.

Feet on the Hips

- Make sure to pull his legs across your front at the same time you move your hips back.
- The path of Blue's hands is as if he was drawing an arch or turning a big wheel.

Blue steps back with his right foot to clear his right hip and begins to pull White's left hand toward him as he pushes White's feet away from him. Blue thrusts his right arm away from himself in an arch-like motion. He wants to spin White 90 degrees, pivoting him on the curve of his back.

Blue continues to pull White's sleeve toward himself as he pushes the legs away. This causes White to spin in place, and makes space for Blue to pass the guard.

Once Blue has cleared White's feet, he immediately steps up with his right foot to the knee-on-belly position. Notice Blue still has control of White's legs and arm.

LEG DRAG TO ARM BAR

This is a variation on the previous technique. If, as you spin your opponent on his back, he leave his arm extended, an armbar is there for the taking.

Blue is standing in White's open guard. White puts his feet on Blue's hips. Blue reaches under White's left ankle with his left hand and grabs the cloth below the knee. Blue also grabs White's right sleeve with his left hand.

Blue steps back with his left foot.

Blue steps back with his right foot, making space between his hips and White's feet. As Blue steps back with his right foot, he simultaneously pulls White's feet toward his right as he pulls White's right arm toward his left, causing White's body to rotate counter clockwise.

Now that he has cleared White's feet, Blue steps forward and goes to the knee-on-belly position. Notice Blue maintains his grips and pulls White's right arm straight up.

Blue steps over White's head with his left foot and lowers his hips, sitting close to White's shoulder as he grabs White's wrist with his right hand.

Blue falls back for the armbar. He uses his leg against White's face to prevent White from sitting up as he sits back.

REVERSE KNEE ON BELLY

◀ Blue grips White's wrist and knee and puts his left knee on White's belly.

REVERSE KNEE ON BELLY
Sometimes you will not be able to get the rear knee in the belly from the leg drag or from other passes. In trying to prevent you from doing so, your opponent may leave an opening for the front knee. This technique exploits those situations.

◀ Blue pushes off his right foot, driving his weight into White as he slides his shin across White's hips.

> Consider switching to regular the normal knee on belly position or side control if you feel them preparing for the spin.

◀ Blue releases his right grip and spins his body to his right, swinging his right leg back over White's head.

> Drill the spin part until you can make the turn smoothly. Be careful not to whack your buddies in the head with your ankle as you come around.

▶ Once he has completed the turn, Blue pulls his right leg in tight to White's side and sits on White's chest.

▶ Blue drops his left knee to the floor and establishes the top mount.

> If your opponent tries to defend by bracing with his arms to keep you from spinning, turn the opposite way, step over, and you have the mount.

142 STANDING PASSES ❖ FEET ON HIPS

Blue stands in White's open guard and holds inside White's knees.

Blue twists his hips to the right and moves his right leg outside White's left foot.

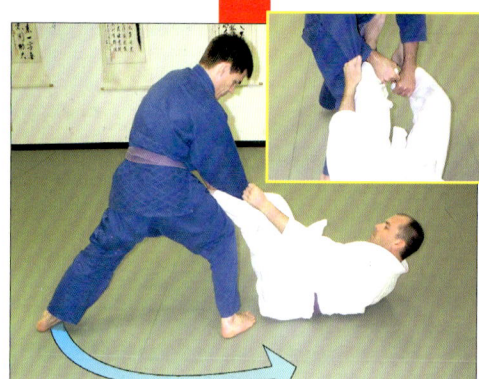

Blue leans his weight into the outside of White's leg as he spins. He will keep contact and pressure on White throughout the turn.

As he completes the spin, Blue lets go with his right hand and drops his hips onto White.

Blue continues turning, bringing his right leg over to establish side control.

SIDEWAYS SPINNING PASS

There is only one way to complete this guard pass: fast and loose. Use the element of surprise, and be careful not to cover too much lateral distance; you do not want to roll past the opponent's head.

> ↻ Blue must momentarily remove the soles of White's feet from his hips. He does so with a combination of footwork, a twist of the hips, and a quick pop of his arms. Blue lets his weight crash down as he turns.
>
> There must be constant weight on, and contact with, the opponent's leg/body throughout the spin. This is to limit the opponent's mobility. It serves the added benefit of giving you feedback as to where he is for the instant that your back is turned.

FEET ON THE HIPS

BACK AND FORTH

Deception is useful for passing the guard. Fake one way then go another.

White has Blue in the open guard, his feet on Blue's hips. Blue holds the cloth inside White's knees.

Blue moves his hips to his left and pushes White's legs to the right side, making White believe he is going to pass around to the right.

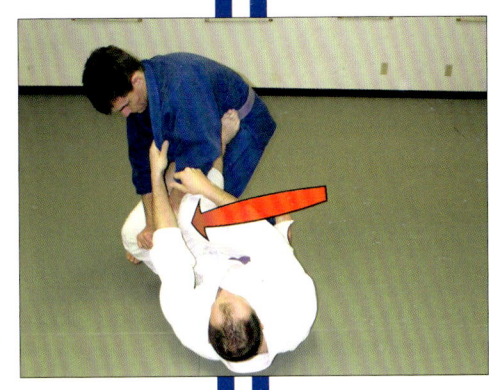

When White resists by pulling his legs to his right, Blue suddenly reverses the force and pushes both of White's legs down to his (White's) right, simultaneously moving around White's left side.

Blue leans all his weight into White and pushes White's legs down to the mat at White's right side.

Blue lowers his body, gets control of the head, and establishes side control.

LASSO PASS

White puts both feet on Blue's hips.

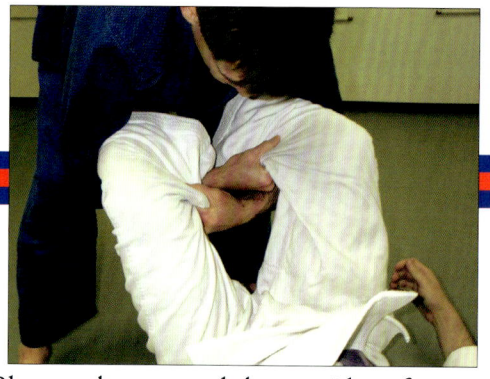

Blue reaches around the outsides of White's legs and grabs the cloth near the knees on both sides.

White's feet are still on Blue's hips at this point.

Blue pulls out with his elbows, squeezing White's legs together.

Blue sprawls back and lays his weight on top of White's legs, turning his head to look to the side.

Keeping his weight down, Blue begins to shuffle his feet around to his left. Blue moves around until he clears White's feet. Blue circles his feet opposite the way he is looking.

This is another guard pass to use when both your opponent's feet are on your hips and you are standing. This technique will work even if your opponent is holding both your sleeves, and that is, in fact, a good time to use it.

> ⓘ If your opponent manages to get to his side after you collapse on his legs, consider following up with the low-mount technique from page 76.

Blue moves his right hand over to under-hook White's right hip and then reaches for head control with his left arm to establish side control.

Step-Through Pass

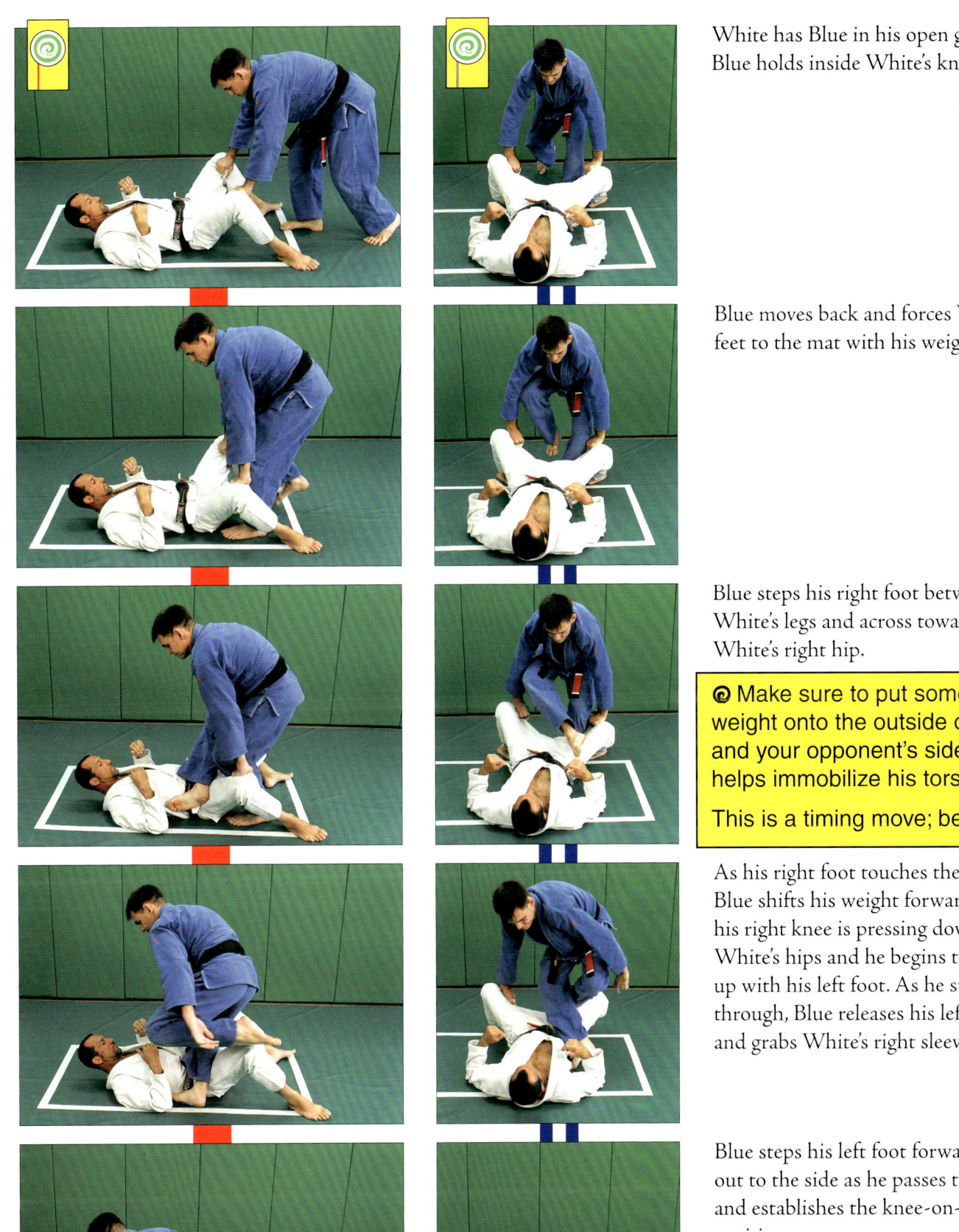

White has Blue in his open guard. Blue holds inside White's knees.

Blue moves back and forces White's feet to the mat with his weight.

Blue steps his right foot between White's legs and across toward White's right hip.

◉ Make sure to put some of your weight onto the outside of your shin and your opponent's side. Doing so helps immobilize his torso.

This is a timing move; be quick.

As his right foot touches the mat, Blue shifts his weight forward so that his right knee is pressing down on White's hips and he begins to step up with his left foot. As he steps through, Blue releases his left grip and grabs White's right sleeve.

Blue steps his left foot forward and out to the side as he passes the guard and establishes the knee-on-belly position.

146 STANDING PASSES ◆ SITTING GUARD

CARTWHEEL PASS

The cartwheel pass requires daring and athleticism. It is seen at advanced levels with and without the gi. Look for it if your opponent is sitting and bent forward and does not have control over either of your legs.

White sits up in open guard.

Blue grabs behind White's collar with his left hand.

Blue leans forward and posts his right hand on the mat between White's feet.

Note the placement of Blue's hand on White's back. When he jumps, most of Blue's weight will be on the floor. He will use the hand on White's back mostly for control and balance.

Here the right hand posts on the mat.

Sitting Guard

Blue pushes off with both feet and springs over White in a cartwheel motion, twisting his body in the air.

Note: it is not necessary to get vertical, as in this picture, to pull off the move.

Blue lands on both feet behind White, and grabs White's chest lapel with his right hand.

Blue falls back to the mat, pulling White back with him as he puts his hooks in to take the back.

This pass can also be done with the right hand posted on the opponent's knee instead of the mat. Obviously, however, the knee is not going to be as stable as the floor.

REVOLVING BACK ATTACK

Here is an interesting one. Instead of passing the guard, White goes straight for Blue's back. This comes in handy against the guard player who is very comfortable bent in half in a collapsed guard. You need to be quick about getting your chest to his back after the spin, and beware of toehold attempts as you get there.

Blue stacks White on his shoulders, pushing White's feet over his head.

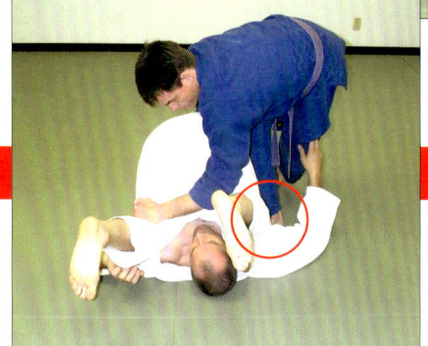

Blue pushes his left palm down on the back of White's left knee to hold him down. At the same time, Blue steps his right foot across to the side of White's right hip.

Blue swings his left foot over White's legs and sits on the back of White's legs.

Blue hooks his right foot over the top of White's right hip and turns to his left, lying down onto his left side. As he turns, Blue grabs the back of White's belt with both hands.

Blue pulls White into him, and then grabs over the top of White's shoulder. Blue pulls White's upper body into him and sets his hooks in.

Blue reaches around White's neck with his free hand and takes White's back completely.

INVERTED GUARD

149

> To prevent being passed, a player will fend with his legs from whatever position necessary. These two techniques address a north/south situation.

White has spun under to prevent the pass. White has lifted his feet over his head and pushes Blue off with both feet on Blue's chest.

In this variation, White has attempted the same defense, bringing his feet back over his head and pushing Blue's chest away.

Blue grabs with both hands, four fingers in, at the sides of White's collar.

Blue lowers his head and grabs underneath White's armpits with both hands.

Using the power of his legs and hips, Blue begins to stand and pull up with his hands.

Blue sprawls his feet back and drives his head into White's gut as he pulls up and in with his hands. Blue pushes out with his elbows to make space.

As Blue pulls White's upper body up off the mat, White's lower body cannot help but drop.

Blue continues driving his head forward and pulling in until he flattens Blue and establishes control.

The instant White's feet hit the floor, Blue quickly drops on top of him and establishes control.

⊚ *Standing to pass is an effective way to open the closed guard; it puts gravity on your side.*

standing up

▶ **One leg at a time:** Minimize the effort needed. Lean one way and lift the leg on the other side. Lean the other way and forward to lift the other leg.

▶ **Both legs at once:** The more you put your weight on your hands, the easier it becomes to pop up onto your feet.

opening closed guard

▶ **Blast out:** The element of surprise is key here. The power of your back is enough to open the legs. Stand up quickly and thrust your hips forward.

▶ **Can opener:** By driving your opponent's head toward his hips, you force him to open guard or be submitted.

▶ **Elbow pressure:** This is similar to using elbow pressure from on the knees. When standing you make pressure into their legs with your lower back, by stepping back.

▶ **Knee-in-the-butt:** Put your knee-cap on their tailbone and step back with your other leg. Your lower back moves back as you step back and lower your hips.

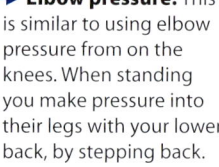    

knee through middle *can be used with a variety of guard opening techniques*

▶ **Combat base:** The knee-in-the-butt guard opener sets up combat base. You can go either way with your lead knee and still pass.

▶ **Combat base:** The knee-in-the-butt guard opener sets up combat base. You can go either way with your lead knee and still pass.

▶ **Cross-grip:** A cross-grip on the opponent's sleeve negates sweeps. Push the knee down then put your own knee over. You are now set up to pass.

     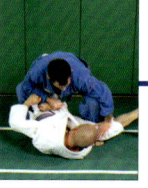 

▶ **Cross-grip:** The smash pass is another option from standing with a cross-grip. This works best if the leg your under-hook has the top ankle.

opening closed guard

▶ **Thrust choke:** Usually you will not get a submission, but it does open their legs. Beware of arm bar attempts.

▶ **Double thrust choke:** As with the thrust choke, the result is opening the legs.

▶ **Ankle attack & counter:** Beware of your opponent grabbing your ankles. If they do, make sure to hold their gi to counter sweep attempts.

▶ **Twist and drop:** Drop your knee into their stomach as you control their hips. When they open their guard, under-hook on the side you dropped your knee.

▶ **No. 2:** Just like from the knees...if the smash pass is blocked, go a different direction, keeping your forward pressure on all the while. (see Ch. 2).

hanging opponent

▶ **Push down on a knee:** As soon a their legs open your knee goes through the middle. Play the smash-pass game (Ch. 2) standing.

▶ **If they won't open the guard:** Push down on a knee and turn to that side. Drop both your knees over their thigh then get an under-hook. Move to kesa-gatame.

▶ **Uncross the ankles:** Figure out which ankle is on top and scoop under that leg. Proceed directly to the smash pass.

ⓒ Once his legs open you can control his hips.

sit on the hips

▶ **Contain the hips:** The insides of your knees pinch the outsides of theirs. Sit on the back of their legs, pick a side, and push their legs to the side.

▶ **Step over pass:** This works well if you contain their hips (above). Be bold and drop all your weight on them as you throw your leg over.

◉ **Get your opponent's feet off your biceps before you pass.**

removing feet from arms

▶ **Use you knee to block:** Get their foot out of your elbow by dropping your elbow past your knee.

▶ **Use you knee to push:** Push your knee into the back of his knee.

▶ **Use you knee to push across:** Coming in from the outside, push your knee into the back of his knee.

▶ **Push hands:** Duck both arms and slide the backs of your hands simultaneously behind back of his lower legs.

▶ **Step on it:** Step on the inside of their thigh, using your foot like a hand. Use posture and your hips to clear his other leg.

▶ **Pt. 1) Inside elbow:** Use the inside of your elbow against the inside of his inner calve. A proper grip is key; you must use it for base and a to pivo your elbow up and under.

▶ **Pt. 2) Use your knee to push:** Same as above but this time your free arm is blocking the leg you already cleared (Pt. 1).

▶ **Duck under:** Your free arm holds his thigh as you make a big step through. Pivot off the back of your neck, not the back of your head.

open guard passes

▶ **Double elbows:** Your free arm holds his thigh as you make a big step through. Pivot off the back of your neck, not the back of your head.

▶ **Jump back then around:** Hop back and push down his knees. Pivot off your arms and circle your lower body.

↻ Get past your opponent's legs, then control his upper body.

▶ **Leapfrog:** Once his feet are on the mat, leapfrog over his knees. Your arms carry your weight, keeping his legs pinned.

  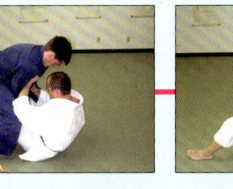 

▶ **Over the top:** Pin one knee to the mat then post your other hand on his other knee and move your hips over then below the knee that is up.

▶ **Body lock:** Use your knee/shin to push the outside of his knee across his body and in front of his other knee. Pull the arm and transition to kesa-gatame.

▶ **Body lock:** Instead of the above, post off the shin that pinning his top knee and jump to his rear.

▶ **Leg drag:** Hold his same side sleeve and pants. Move your hips then lift and simultaneously spin him, go knee on belly.

▶ **Arm bar:** From the knee-on-belly position you may find a good opening to move to the juji-gatame.

▶ **Reverse knee on belly:** Sometimes you have a better chance to pin down his hips if you use the opposite knee. The position is not stable so spin to mount.

▶ **Spin pass:** As you spin, make sure that your torso is always in contact with the opponent. Land chest to chest.

▶ **Back and forth:** Fake one way then go the other. Be ready to follow up.

▶ **Lasso grip:** Wrap your arms under and grab cloth around his shins. Drop your chest on his knees and circle.

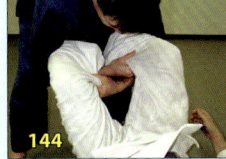   

feet on the ground

▶ **Step through pass:** As you step through post the outside of your shin against his hip. This sticks his hips as you move over.

▶ **Cartwheel pass:** Post on the floor and the back of his neck. Immediately attack his back.

inverted guard

▶ **Revolving back attack:** Control his hips then change grips. Take a big step over then quickly tie up his upper body.

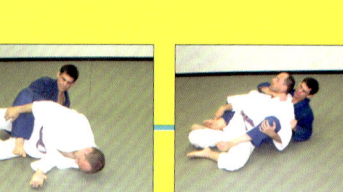

▶ **Use your head:** Counter the inverted guard by forcing down his hips with your head.

▶ **Lift the snake by its head:** Lift the lapels. When his head comes up his feet have to come down. Drop your chest down at that moment.

Chapter 4

DEFENSES AND COUNTERS TO COMMON ATTACKS:

While attempting to pass your opponent's guard, you must always be on guard against attacks. Your opponent should be continuously attempting to submit or sweep you. The most important element of the guard pass is to maintain your balance at all times. Because of the dynamic nature of the guard fight, you will need to make constant adjustments in position, grips, and center of gravity. It is also important to understand which offensive techniques are available to your opponent from various positions and grips. The best time to stop an attack is as early as possible. Remaining aware of your opponent's position, movement, and grips will allow you to adjust your own position to your advantage before you are caught in a threatening situation. The best way to develop the sensitivity necessary to maintain your base while passing the guard is through sparring drills. In most BJJ academies, a great deal of time is spent on practicing the techniques of attacking from and passing the guard.

Once you are caught in a disadvantageous position or the opponent has caught you in a submission technique you will need to apply a defensive technique, and possibly a counter-offensive of your own. Although stopping your opponent's attack as early as possible is best, sometimes you will find yourself 'caught' in a submission attempt. There are specific guidelines and techniques designed to handle these types of situations. It is important to practice these escapes and counters from disadvantageous positions on a regular basis. Once you have successfully defended your opponent's attack, you ideally will continue with a counter-offensive technique. You may move from a defensive technique into a guard pass, or into a submission technique of your own (most often leg attacks). It bears repeating that maintaining a solid base and adjusting to keep your balance as necessary is the best way to avoid being caught by the opponent's attack.

156 DEFENSES AND COUNTERS ◆ GRIPS ON THE KNEE

GRIPS ON THE KNEE

If your opponent can get a good grip on the outside of your knee using your gi pants, you need to be cautious. He will be looking to sweep you with the aid of that grip. Break the grip before you pass and you will avoid a lot of problems.

ATTACK

White grabs the cloth on the outside of Blue's right knee.

White uses the leverage of his grip to break Blue's posture. A sweep for White is now imminent.

DEFENSE 1

White grabs the cloth on the outside of Blue's right knee.

Blue immediately grabs over the top of White's left wrist with his right hand.

Blue pulls up on White's wrist to break his grip on the pants.

DEFENSE 2

Blue can also grab over the top of White's left wrist...

...and force White's left hand to the mat as he simultaneously kicks his right leg back, breaking White's grip.

Arm-wrap

Arm-wrap

The arm-wrap is a pesky situation for the guard passer. It provides a number of choke and armlock options for the guard player. For the most part, you need to free yourself of the arm-wrap before you do much else.

Attack

Bad for Blue: White has trapped Blue's right arm by wrapping his own left arm around it and then anchoring his left hand by feeding the gi to it with his right hand. Blue is in danger of chokes and attacks against his right arm.

Defense

White wraps Blue's left arm tightly, preparing to attack.

Blue leans to his right, rolls his left shoulder over and lifts his right elbow. Notice how Blue rotates his shoulder forward and across as he twists his lower arm to the rear.

Pulling up sharply with his left elbow, Blue jerks his arm free.

Blue neutralizes White's collar grip, and at the same time he controls White's leg.

> ⊙ A general rule is that anytime your arm gets trapped under your opponent's back, you free it by moving it towards his feet, not toward his head.

Guillotine

The guillotine is a very effective submission and one that even beginners know to some degree. You must know how to defend it. Your best defense to the guillotine is to stay out of it in the first place. From inside the guard, maintaining good posture will prevent the guillotine. Should you get caught, however, a back-up plan will be needed. Here is a late defense. As you apply the defense, realize that, first and foremost, you need to survive. Improve your position incrementally while keeping the pressure on your opponent. Find space in your opponent's hold and position your carotid arteries into that space to take the pressure off of them. You need to keep your wits about you, and it takes practice. Eventually most opponents will fatigue and let go.

White sits up and wraps his right arm around Blue's neck.

White grabs his right wrist with his left hand and falls back to lock his guard and finish the choke. As White falls back, Blue wraps his right arm around White's neck.

Blue pulls down on White's shoulder and pushes the other way with his head.

Blue sprawls onto the balls of his feet and walks forward as far as he can, squeezing White's neck and pressing his right shoulder into White's throat. White will not have enough leverage to finish the choke. It is very important to continue driving forward and press the weight into the opponent's throat.

Blue walks his feet up as far as possible and smashes his weight into White's throat to defend the choke. Blue can also use his free arm to take off White's arm. This may be necessary if White is stubborn with the hold.

X Choke Defenses

As with the guillotine, the best defense against the X-choke and most of its variations is posture. Good posture prevents the initial grip your opponent needs to start the choke, for the most part. But as you grapple, your posture will sometimes be compromised, and your opponent will get dangerous grips against you. The next three pages show techniques for nullifying or escaping lapel grips used to choke.

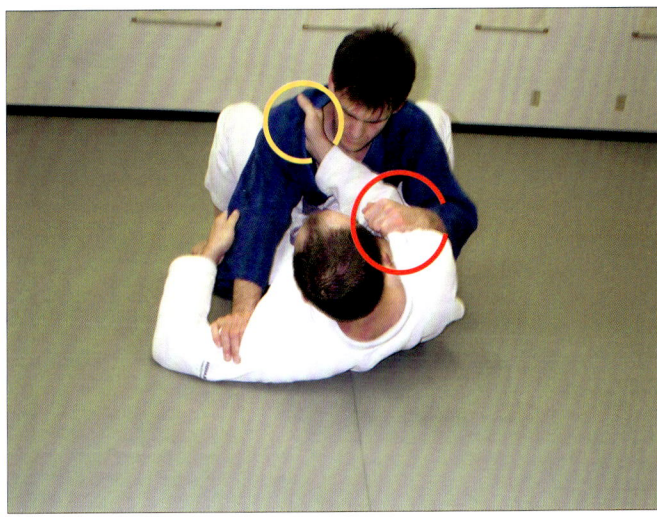

White puts his right hand inside Blue's right lapel to set up a cross choke. Blue immediately holds down White's free arm with his right hand to prevent the completion of the choke.

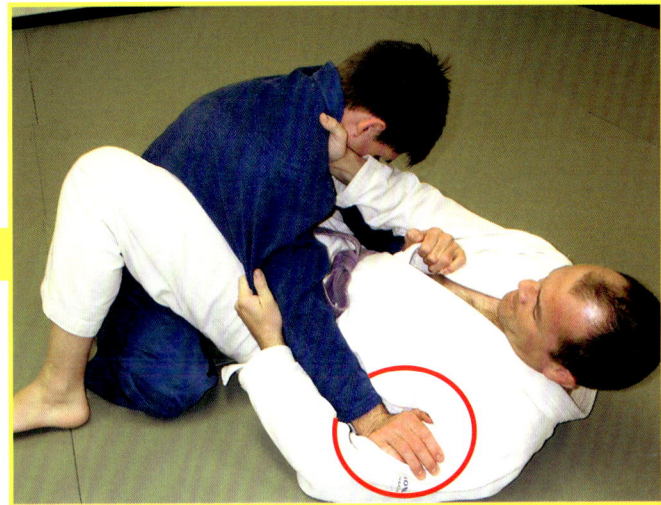

View from the other side: White cannot finish the choke with one arm. Blue needs to be wary of White switching to an attack of his right arm.

White sets up for a cross choke. Blue pulls down on White's left arm with his right hand, first to prevent White from getting the grip he wants and then to prevent him from drawing his elbow outwards.

Blue tucks his chin down against his chest to protect his neck.

As White sets his first grip, Blue slides his right hand up inside White's wrist. This takes pressure off the carotid artery, thus killing the choke. Here, Blue also pushes White's right elbow away and across his body. This relieves pressure also.

Some opponents generate enough power to finish chokes even if you have put your own hand in for defense; they can choke you with pressure through your own hand. Pushing the elbow helps prevent this.

This is a cross choke defense if the opponent already has the cross-grip position. White sets the choke. Blue pulls down on White's lower (left) elbow with his right hand and pushes White's top (right) elbow away with his left hand to make space between white's arms.

Blue continues to pull down with his right hand and push away with his left. Blue has killed the choke at this point. If White won't let go, Blue can pass his head through the space between White's arms or protect with his hand as in the next frame.

Blue threads his right hand between White's arms and reaches his right palm up beside the right side of his head to protect his neck.

Chokes

White puts his right hand inside Blue's right lapel to set up a cross choke. Blue immediately holds down White's free arm with his right hand to prevent the completion of the choke.

Blue slides his left hand up under White's right armpit. Blue levers up a little off of his own wrist to raise White's elbow, allowing space for Blue to duck his head under.

Blue ducks his head and circles it to his right underneath White's wrist to remove the threat of the cross choke.

Blue has now "uncrossed" White's grip, extricating himself in the process.

Attack

Blue grabs inside White's right lapel with his right hand, four fingers in.

Blue brings his left leg over to the left side of White's neck. Blue pulls with his right hand and pushes with his left leg, choking White.

Defense

White attempts to choke Blue as described above. Blue grabs his right lapel with his right hand.

Blue jerks his lapel out of White's grip, releasing the choke.

Armbars (Juji-Gatame)

ARMBARS

Before an opponent can take your arm, he must establish a position to do so. You can prevent armbars—or any other type of submission—by preventing your opponent from putting together the elements necessary for his attack. For instance, before the armbar can be successfully applied, the attacker will need to move his hips in the direction of the arm he is attacking. If the player on top adjusts his base immediately so that he remains centered with the attacker, the attack will fail.

◀ Blue shows a correct method of holding the opponent for an **armbar from the Guard:**
- ❖ Blue's hips are high under White's right armpit.
- ❖ The fulcrum of Blue's leverage is above White's elbow joint.
- ❖ Blue pinches his knees together.
- ❖ Blue keeps pressure on White's head with the back of his left leg.
- ❖ Blue's body is at approximately a 90-degree angle to White's.
- ❖ Blue holds White's wrist with both hands (there is a variety of ways to hold the arm).
- ❖ White's thumb points away from Blue's chest.
- ❖ Blue raises his hips to finish the move.

◀ Close-up of the hand position:
- ❖ Blue holds the wrist at the juncture of the wrist and palm, making it difficult for White to rotate his arm away from the pressure.
- ❖ Blue also keeps his elbows locked tight to his sides for more power.

Here is an example of the principle discussed above. As White pulls Blue's right arm in to set up an armbar, Blue moves his left arm inside White's leg in anticipation of the coming attack.

As White pulls Blue's right arm across his chest, Blue braces it against being pulled across his body with his other arm. Even if White gets Blue's right arm where he wants it, the position of Blue's elbow next to White's left thigh prevents White from squeezing his knees together and performing the attack.

White controls Blue's right arm and brings his right leg high, pushing inward to break Blue's posture.

As White attempts to bring his left leg over Blue's head, Blue catches behind White's lower leg with his left hand.

> ⊘ By denying necessary elements of the submission, Blue defeats it. White needs to wrap his left leg around Blue's head and then squeeze his knees together. Blue does let that happen. White's armbar attempt turns into a guard-passing opportunity for Blue.

Blue pulls White's left leg down and across.

Blue smashes his weight onto White's legs to control his hips and frees his arm.

With his arms free and both of Whites legs to one side, Blue has all but passed White's guard.

Armbars (Juji-gatame)

165

White sets up the armbar. Blue is ready and immediately begins his defense. He starts by opening his hand.

 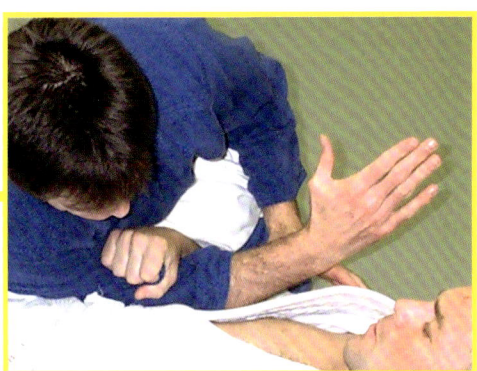

White begins to pass his leg over Blue's head. Blue puts his right palm on his left biceps and bends his left arm to prevent his right arm from straightening.

 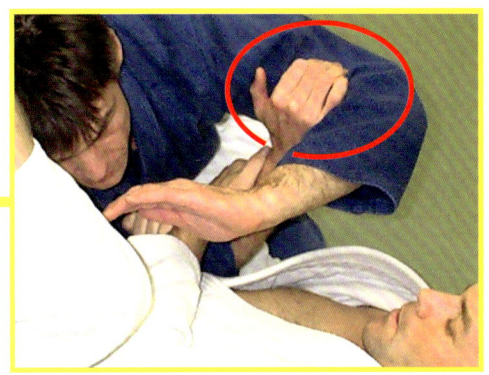

As White passes his left leg over Blue's head, Blue pushes down with his left palm on the back of White's leg. As Blue pushes down on White's leg, he also lowers down his upper body, using his weight to smash down White's leg.

 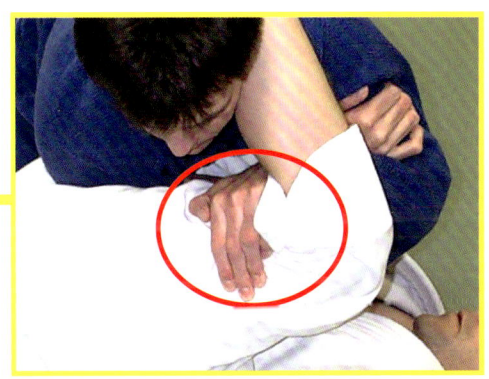

Blue smashes all his weight onto White's legs, pushing White's knees into his face and raising his hips off the ground.

Give to get: An effective gambit, using this technique, is to bait your opponent into attempting the armbar and when he does, using this defense. From the position at the end of the sequence, Blue is almost past White's guard. All Blue needs to do is move to White's left side and keep up the forward pressure. Basically, Blue will follow up by using the smash pass.

Blue keeps his weight down and maintains the downward pressure behind White's left leg as he jerks his right arm free. He pulls the elbow out in sudden and forceful spurts, inching it out if need be.

166 Defenses and Counters ❖ Armbars (Juji-gatame)

1. This variation is used when the opponent has the armbar almost completely set up. White catches Blue's right arm in an armbar.

2. Blue hooks his right hand inside his left elbow crook to keep White from straightening the elbow.

3. Blue drives forward and stacks White onto his shoulders, lifting White's hips off the ground. Blue simultaneously lays his upper body weight onto the back of White's legs to prevent him from straightening his legs and hips. Blue his left knee beside White's head and puts his right knee up behind White's hips, preventing White from moving his hips.

4. Keeping his weight down, Blue works his left hand up between White's legs and hooks his palm over the back of White's left thigh.

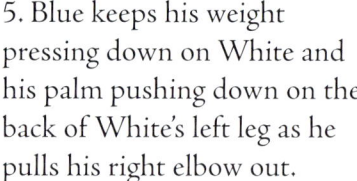

5. Blue keeps his weight pressing down on White and his palm pushing down on the back of White's left leg as he pulls his right elbow out.

6. Blue pulls his right arm free, while keeping his weight down on White's legs.

Use this technique instead of the last one when it is too late to thread your arm behind the opponent's leg from the beginning.

7. Blue reaches across with his right hand and grabs White's right collar, thumb-inside.

8. Blue moves around to his right while he presses down on White's throat, passing the guard.

Armbars (Juji-gatame)

White catches Blue's right arm in an armbar.

Blue grabs behind White's neck with his left hand.

Blue smashes his weight down onto White, pulling himself down with is left hand and forcing White's knees into his face. At the same time, Blue slides his left knee near White's head and puts his right knee up behind White's hips.

Keeping his weight down, Blue begins to pull his right elbow backward.

Blue frees his right arm.

Blue pushes White's legs across to his left with his right hand (pushing outside White's left knee).

Blue moves around to his right and passes White's guard.

More give to get: The techniques on this spread are more examples of techniques you can bait your opponent with in order to set up a guard pass.

168 DEFENSES AND COUNTERS ❖ ARMBARS (JUJI-GATAME)

LATE DEFENSE TO AN ARMBAR

This is a last ditch defense. Use it when your opponent goes belly down in his attempt to apply an armbar. When he does go belly down, there will be a moment when it is difficult for him to keep the leg over your head (White's left in the pictures) tight. Use that moment to push away that leg with your free hand. The space you create allows you to move your head one way and the rest of your body another. You need to act quickly. Practice this move with a cooperating partner, and get the timing and movement down before trying it live. When you do use this escape, be bold; you will fail if you hesitate.

White catches Blue's right arm in an armbar.

Blue brings his weight forward and smashes White to prevent White from extending his hips.

White counters by extending and rolling face down for an armbar.

Blue jumps over White's body.

Blue lands on White's left side.

Blue immediately grabs the back of White's neck with his left hand and grabs around the inside of White's left leg with his right arm.

Here is another view of the spinning part of the escape.

White pivots underneath Blue and continues the pressure with a face-down armbar. Blue twists his right arm thumb up to relieve the pressure on his elbow.

Armbars (Juji-gatame)

Blue quickly shuffles his feet to his right.

Blue spreads his base and drives forward into side control.

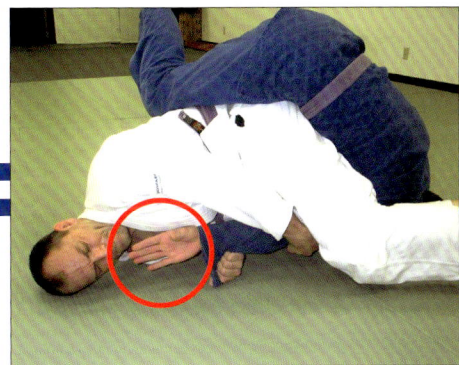

Blue twists his right thumb upward to relieve the pressure on his elbow.

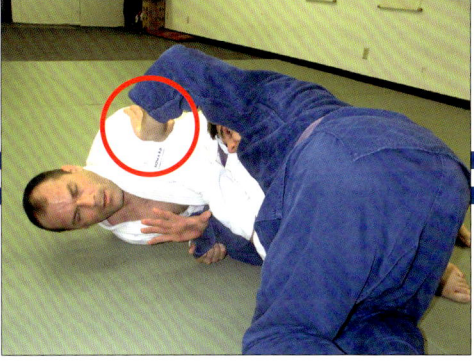

Blue follows through by coming around 270 degrees. Note how he pushes with his free hand to help him come around.

Blue follows through by pushing White onto his back and taking control of White's head.

Defenses and Counters — Double Under-Hook Counter

Attack

White attempts to pass Blue's guard with double under-hooks. Blue scoots his hips back and grabs White's left wrist with his right hand.

Blue inserts his right foot all the way across White's hips. The grip on White's wrist is key. Blue pins it to his hip and pulls up on it.

Blue hooks his right foot on the outside of White's right hip. Blue straightens his right leg for a shoulder lock submission.

From this view you can see how Blue hooks his instep on the outside of White's hip. This is necessary to prevent White from turning out of the attack.

Defense

Blue counters the above technique by grabbing White's right ankle and preventing him from hooking it on his right hip.

Omo plata

The omo plata is a great submission when the gi is involved. Without the gi it still is effective, but it is much harder for the attacking player to prevent the defending one from just yanking out his arm. With the gi, a grip on the defender's sleeve end usually prevents that simple defense. If, however, the attacker grips the wrist, or the defender has enough space to snap into the defense, yanking out the arm works.

Blue is caught in omo plata. Blue posts his right foot on the mat and raises his body.

Using the force of his legs and back, Blue rips his arm free.

Most of the time you cannot just yank out your arm, and you probably shouldn't try. Instead, you will need to reposition yourself relative to your opponent to take away the danger. The next five techniques are variations on that approach. As is always the case, the early defenses are the most reliable.

Blue is caught in omo plata. Blue posts his right hand to keep White from forcing him onto his face.

Blue posts his right foot on the mat.

Pushing off his right foot, Blue postures up.

Unable to rip his left arm free, Blue begins to turn into White.

Blue pushes White's left leg away with his right hand, opening White's legs and controlling his hips.

Blue turns into White's guard, effectively releasing the pressure on his left arm.

With the last two omo plata escapes, Blue had a chance to posture and escape. Suppose now that the opponent forces down his shoulder. Blue's first option, if White does not control his hips, is simply to go with the flow and roll out of the submission. This only works if White does not control his hips early on, which is fundamental to the technique. The fact of the matter is, in the heat of battle, players make mistakes. You need to recognize those mistakes and exploit them, which is what Blue does on this page.

On the next page are two escapes for situations where the opponent does make an effort to prevent the rolling escape on this page. Granted, White does not have solid control over Blue's hips in these instances. If he did, Blue would use the technique on the next spread.

Blue is caught in omo plata.

Unable to posture up, Blue posts his right hand on the mat and turns his head away from White as he lowers his left shoulder to the mat.

Blue pushes off with his feet and begins to roll forward over his left shoulder.

As Blue completes the roll, he begins to turn in towards White.

Blue comes up on his left hip.

Continuing, Blue turns over onto his knees.

> ⊙ Blue always rolls over the shoulder of the arm that is trapped when using this escape.

Omo Plata

Blue is caught in omo plata, White also has **control of Blue's left leg**.

> Use this escape when your opponent holds around your knee or thigh instead of your hip.

Blue posts his right hand on the mat and begins to slide his left knee up over White's chest.

Blue lifts his hips and posts his left foot on the mat. He uses the ball of his foot for base and then puts his knee on White's chest.

Blue drops his left knee into White's chest and lifts his left foot over White's head. Blue brings his left leg to the other side of White as soon as White lets go.

Pushing off with his right foot, Blue jumps over to White's left side.

Blue lands in side control on White's left side.

White sets up the shoulder lock, **holding Blue's belt.** Blue grabs his belt to defend.

Blue lifts his left leg and begins to slide it over the top of White's chest.

Blue slides his leg over White and drops his left knee on White's left side.

Blue sits up in his base and uses his legs and back to straighten up and pull his left arm free.

174 DEFENSES AND COUNTERS ❖ OMO PLATA

LATE ESCAPES FROM THE OMO PLATA

These are omo plata escapes that work even if your opponent sits up and manages to wrap his arm around your waist. That is how it is shown in the bottom photo sequence. In the top set of photos, White does not have a good grip on Blue's belt. But even if he did, the execution of the escape by Blue would be the same. In the top example, Blue grabs White's attacking leg (the right) and holds it as he shoots under. To make that work, Blue has to make the grip on White's leg with the same arm he uses to post. He posts on his elbow to make that possible.

Blue is caught in the omo plata.

Blue posts his right elbow to the mat and extends his left leg backward. Blue will post on his right elbow and opposite (left) foot to move his hips.

Blue slides his right knee underneath his left leg.

In this variation, Blue grabs White's other (left) leg as he turns under White. An advantage to this approach is that it is easier for Blue to post with his right arm. A disadvantage is that the alternate grip gives him less control over White, and so White is not turned around the extra half rotation seen in the version above.

White attacks with the omo plata. Blue grabs his belt to stop White from finishing him quickly.

Because White is controlling Blue's hips with his right arm, Blue is unable to roll forward to escape. Blue grabs his belt to defend the leverage.

Blue begins to slide onto his right hip.

Omo Plata

> Blue posts on his foot and hand to facilitate swinging his body underneath White. The action is like a pendulum. It is important that Blue generate a bit of momentum. Blue must also pull White across as he goes under.

Blue lays down on his right side and begins to slide his hips underneath White as he simultaneously begins to pull White over the top of him.

Blue turns onto his left hip as he continues pulling White over him.

Blue comes up over White's side. He moves his hips back toward the camera as he does. Blue will go to his knees from here, scissoring his legs if necessary to get there.

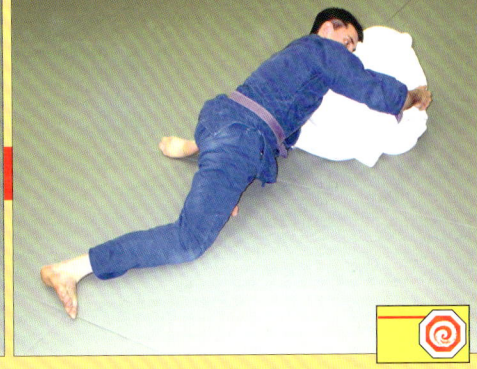

Blue rolls to his left, pulling White over his body and sliding his right knee underneath White's right hip. Blue grabs White's pants to move his leg.

White lands on Blue's left side. Blue changes his grip to help pull himself up.

Blue comes up and rolls White into side control.

Attack

▶ White is in Blue's open guard. Blue controls White's right sleeve and hooks his right ankle over White's right hip.

▶ Blue wraps his left leg over the top of White's right arm, inserting his left ankle into White's elbow crook.

▶ As White begins to pass around to Blue's right side, Blue triangles his legs, his left ankle hooked behind his right knee. Blue pulls tight on White's arm.

▶ As White passes around the right side of Blue's guard, Blue reaches up with both hands around White's upper arm and pulls down with both hands as he drops his left knee toward the mat for a keylock on White's right arm.

▶ Close-up of the leg position from the other side.

Defense

▶ White catches Blue's arm in a keylock.

▶ Blue moves back into White's guard, posts his right foot for base, and grabs around White's left leg with his left arm, pulling White's leg up so that White cannot apply downward pressure with his leg.

▶ Blue pulls White's left knee up and in.

▶ Blue pulls his right arm free.

▶ Blue is now safe to pass the guard.

Biceps Crush/Keylock

Defense

▶ White catches Blue's right arm in a keylock.

▶ Blue's arm goes behind White's neck and his right arm lifts White's lower body stacking White up onto his shoulders.

▶ Blue smashes White, laying his weight onto White's chest. Blue is using his right knee to take away White's ability to move his hips. **This is vital.**

▶ With his thumb in the back of White's collar, Blue circles his left elbow around White's head.

▶ Blue holds White's hips off the mat and crushes his throat with his left forearm.

178 DEFENSES AND COUNTERS ❖ TRIANGLE (SANGAKU-JIME)

> Remember, the best defense is to prevent the submission attempt from ever becoming a serious threat. This is a good first option against the triangle.

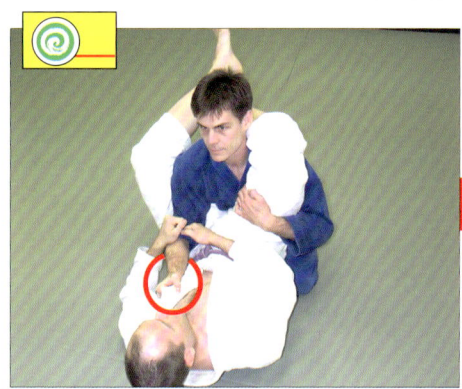

White begins to set up a triangle choke. Blue reacts by anchoring his right hand and assuming a solid, upright posture.

Blue immediately grabs the inside of White's right leg and pulls outward. At the same time, Blue straightens his back and lifts his head high.

Blue pushes upward with his hips, lifting his rear off his heels, and breaks the hold.

Earlier in the chapter, we talked about baiting the opponent to attempt an armbar to set up a guard pass. The same thing can be done with the triangle, and this defense is a good technique from which to pass. In the photos, White manages to get his foot behind his knee, and then Blue passes. You do not want that to happen. Start your defense as soon as possible to prevent your opponent from locking up his triangle; this will make things easier for you. Once you escape, proceed with the smash pass.

White closes the triangle.

Blue immediately sprawls onto his toes and smashes his weight into White's left leg as he moves around to White's left side. The pressure opens White's legs.

Blue continues to smash all his weight into White as he drives his head forward over White's head.

Blue grabs White's right lapel with his left hand and brings his left knee up behind White's hips to control White's movement.

Blue pulls White's right lapel open as he feeds his left hand deep into the right side of White's collar, thumb in.

Blue smashes his weight onto White as he pulls up with his left hand and drives his right elbow toward the mat, crushing White's throat for the submission.

TRIANGLE (SANGAKU-JIME)

Blue gets caught in a triangle choke that is locked on tight. Blue pulls outward on White's right leg to relieve some of the pressure.

Blue thrusts his body forward and towards his left, putting pressure on the inside of White's right leg. The move should be sudden and forceful.

Blue continues to drive his chest forward and pulls outward on White's right leg to open White's feet.

Blue is caught in a tight triangle. He grabs White's right leg and pulls outward with his left hand.

Blue turns his body to his left and begins to push into White's legs.

Blue pushes off his feet and drives his weight into White's legs at a perpendicular angle (Blue's and White's torsos are 90 degrees to each other). The pressure unlocks White's feet.

Blue drives forward and passes the guard.

180 DEFENSES AND COUNTERS ◆ TRIANGLE (SANGAKU-JIME)

White locks the triangle choke on Blue.

The techniques on this page are ones to use when you are in trouble because your opponent has locked up the triangle and has a good angle for finishing the choke. That is another way of saying that they are late defenses. They are effective, but they are not plan A.

If you succeed with the technique on this page, immediately transition to a knee-through-the-middle (combat base) type pass.

If you succeed with the technique on the next page, scramble to get on top right away, and beware of attacks against your arm.

Blue pulls out on White's right leg with his left hand and begins to stand.

Blue puts his right knee directly in the center of White's rear.

Blue places his left foot behind his right and squats down which wedges his right knee up between White's legs.

◉ The idea here is to use your body weight and leverage to wedge in a kneecap. As Blue sits back, most of his weight is on his right leg. The left leg is used for stability. Bringing in the kneecap has the effect of opening the opponent's legs and relieving pressure on the neck.

As Blue drives his right knee up and lifts his head, the pressure of his right leg wedging between White's legs causes White's legs to open.

TRIANGLE (SANGAKU-JIME)

White catches Blue in a triangle choke.

Blue hugs White's right leg with his right hand to protect his arm and grabs White's right sleeve with his left hand as he stands.

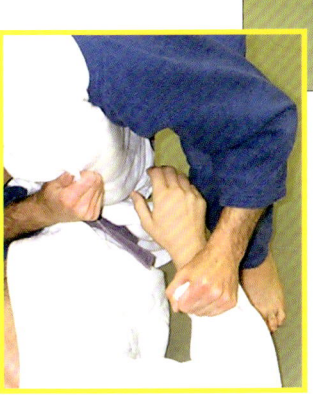

Blue steps his left foot on top of White's right arm.

Blue's leg pushes off White's arm into the mat as he lies down and back to his side. At the same time he pulls White's leg off of his head.

Blue sits on his hip and pulls his head out of the choke.

Blue frees his head. He must immediately be ready if White attempts to switch to an attack against the arm still between White's legs.

182 Defenses and Counters ♦ Triangle (Sangaku-jime)

Blue is caught in a triangle choke.

This is another late defense. Like the last technique, you need to take care of your arm after you escape the triangle. You may wind up on the bottom after using this defense, but at least you have survived.

Blue stands, moves to his left, and hooks his hand over the side of White's neck.

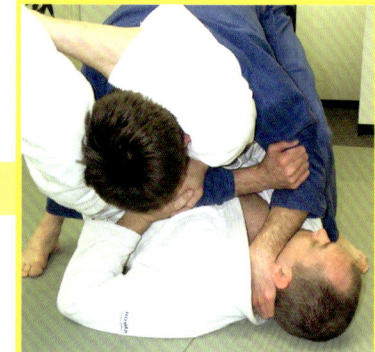

Blue steps over White's head.

Blue sits back and straightens his body. Blue uses his leg to put pressure on White's neck as he does so.

Blue hugs White's right leg tightly to prevent the armbar as he pushes White's head away with his leg and arches his body back to break the triangle.

◉ Blue must be wary of a follow-up armbar attempt.

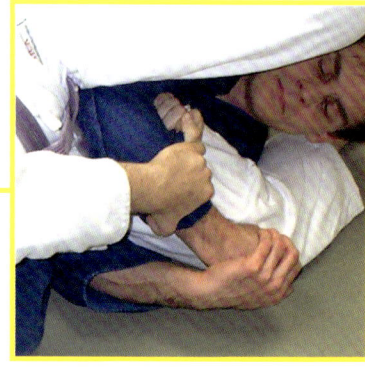

Kimura

Take the Back vs. Kimura

This is a great counter to the Kimura… but only if your timing is adequate. As your opponent goes for the **Kimura**, there is an open path to his back. The only thing in the way is one of his knees. If you can work your way over that knee before he wraps up the figure-four, you will have turned your defense into an attack.

White grabs Blue's right wrist and sits up to hook up a *Kimura*.

White reaches over the top of Blue's elbow with his right arm.

White grabs his own wrist locking on the figure-four grip. Blue grabs White's belt with his right hand to defend the *Kimura* as he drives forward and begins to push down on White's right knee with his left hand.

Continuing to drive forward, Blue steps his left foot forward.

Blue pressures White by pressing the right side of his head behind Blue's right shoulder as he steps his left foot over White's right leg.

Blue turns the corner moving clockwise behind White. Posting his left palm of the mat for base, Blue slides his left knee close behind White's hips. As Blue turns to face White's back, he hooks his right foot over White's right hip.

Blue pulls White backward with his right hand. He lays back and lifts his left foot to over White's left hip.

Blue now has both hooks in and completes taking White's back.

184 DEFENSES AND COUNTERS ❖ KIMURA

From the Half Guard

White sits up and grabs Blue's left wrist with his right hand; he intends to attempt a Kimura.

White reaches over Blue's left arm with his left arm and grabs his own right wrist, trapping Blue's arm.

As White lies back to the mat and attempts to pull Blue's left arm behind his back for a shoulder lock, Blue immediately grabs his own belt to protect his arm.

From the Guard

In this sequence, Blue attempts a similar defense.

Instead of reaching through and grabbing his trapped arm with his free one, Blue grabs his own gi.

Kimura

Blue leans his weight onto White, smashing White's right upper arm to the mat and restricting White's motion and power.

Continuing the downward pressure, Blue presses his weight forward and begins to pull his right hand through to the front of his hips. Blue grabs his own left wrist with his right hand and pulls his arm through.

If White does not pull his arm free, he will be submitted with a shoulder crank.

Blue continues pulling his left wrist up and through with his right hand, causing White's left arm to bend backward until he abandons his grip or submits.

Blue uses his free hand for base and begins to straighten himself up.

Blue switches the free hand to White's hip. He is pushing his torso both forward and up. A good deal of the pressure on White is transmitted through the top of Blue's right shoulder.

If White does not let go, he will get submitted.

This variation is not as effective as the half-guard version. The leverage is not as good.

Defenses and Counters ❖ Hip-Bump Sweep

The hip-bump sweep is a common attack from the guard. Part of any defense is understanding the attack. Stop the bump to stop the sweep.

▶ Blue holds White in his closed Guard. Blue pulls down on White's collar and waits for him to resist backward.

▶ As White pulls back, Blue follows the motion and begins to sit up, posting on his left elbow and opening his feet as he pulls his right foot back. He then reaches over the top of White's right shoulder with his right arm.

▶ As White begins to sit up and sweep, Blue immediately leans forward and pushes White back down with his right hand.

▶ White is pushed back onto the mat. It is important to push the opponent down with the hand on the side to which the opponent attempts to sweep (ex: if the opponent attempts to sweep you to your right side, push him down with your right hand).

▶ Continuing the momentum, Blue raises his hips and posts on his left palm and right foot. He begins to twist to his left.

▶ White has already sat up and reached over Blue's shoulder. Blue leans forward and locks his arms around White's body.

▶ Blue's hips knock White's torso. The movement is forward and in a circle to Blue's left.

▶ Blue drives off his knees and twists to his left.

▶ Blue lands in the mount.

▶ Blue drives White down to the mat.

Hip-Bump Sweep 187

▶ In this variation, White is even further into the sweep. Blue drives forward, hugs White's body with his right arm, and pushes down on the inside of White's right knee.

▶ Blue continues to drive his weight forward.

▶ Blue pushes White's right leg down and begins to bring his left knee up and over White's right leg.

▶ Blue continues to push forward, driving his left knee to the mat over White's right leg.

If Blue gets his knee over, he will be in a good position to pass.

188 DEFENSES AND COUNTERS ❖ SWEEPS VS. STANDING

Attack

White stands up in Blue's guard.

Blue hooks around the inside of White's right leg with his left arm as he posts his right hand over his head.

Blue moves his left hip inside White's right knee.

Blue pushes off with his right hand and begins to push his hips into White's inside right knee.

Defense

Blue stands in White's guard. White sets up the take down as described above.

Blue twists his hips to the left and drives his right knee into White's chest. This prevents White from bridging into Blue's right leg. Blue's left hand holds the inside of White's right knee.

Blue continues to twist his hips and drive his knee down. The pressure breaks White's guard open.

Blue drops his weight onto White. Blue now can swim his right hand behind White's left knee.

Sweeps vs. Standing

The pressure causes Blue to fall onto his back.

Blue continues up to the mount position.

Defense 2

This one is pretty simple, and pretty simple is good; it's easy to remember. Just step out of a hold around your ankle. The key here is to step out early, while you still can.

Blue reaches his right arm around White's left leg and drives his hips downward, clearing White's feet. The pass is essentially the smash pass.

Blue moves into side control.

190 Defenses and Counters ❖ Double Ankle Pick Sweep

Blue is in White's guard.

Blue stands.

As Blue stands up to break the guard, White reaches forward for Blue's ankles.

White grabs behind Blue's ankles and opens his guard.

White extends his legs and pushes Blue backwards. As Blue falls, he turns onto his left side and swings his right leg over the top of White's right leg, putting his right foot on the front of White's right hip.

Blue wraps White's left ankle with his right arm.

Blue grabs his right wrist with his left hand and pulls up as he arches back for the straight ankle lock.

Be sure to pinch your knees tightly when applying the ankle lock.

De la Riva Guard

- De la Riva-style attacks require sleeve grips and/or a grip on the back.
- Prevent the grips to stop the attacks. Here White has good grips.
- There are many opportunities for Blue to attack White's leg. Here Blue is using his arms as base and to keep White from sitting up and transitioning into a leg attack.

White has inserted his right leg through Blue's legs. Blue pushes White's left knee down to the mat by lowering his weight.

Blue grabs White's right ankle with his right hand.

Blue steps his right foot back and pushes White's right ankle down, clearing his right leg.

Blue immediately steps his right leg over the top of White's left leg and drives his left knee over the top of White's hip to pass.

De la Riva

White has his left leg inserted between Blue's legs in the de la Riva guard. Blue reaches down and grabs under White's left heel with his right hand.

Blue reinforces his grip by grabbing under White's left heel with his left hand.

Maintaining a stable position, Blue pulls up with both hands, twisting White's left ankle outward.

White is forced to retract his foot to avoid the submission.

As White pulls his hook out from between Blue's legs, Blue squats and pushes White's foot down to the mat.

Blue continues, driving his right knee over Blue's legs to pass the guard.

Butterfly Guard

Attack

- Blue prepares to attack with a sweep from the **butterfly guard**:
- Blue has both feet hooked inside White's legs.
- Blue has one arm (or both) under White's arm(s), holding his belt at the rear.
- Blue's other hand is holding over White's arm.
- Blue is off-center of White, his weight sits mostly to one side (his right).

Defense

White sits up into the butterfly guard and grips Blue. White under-hooks with his left arm.

Blue pummels his right arm inside and underneath White's left arm.

Blue's under-hooks takes away most of the advantages of White's position.

White puts both hooks inside Blue's legs, sits up, and locks his arms around Blue's body in an underarm bear hug. This is a bad position for Blue.

Blue is in danger of being swept and so must move to a more stable position. As White leans back to sweep, Blue follows and puts his palms under White's chin.

Blue arches his back and pushes White's chin, causing White's head to turn to his right.

Blue continues to push White's chin away as he moves his hips back, breaking the waist lock.

Butterfly Guard

White sits up to the butterfly guard position. Blue grabs behind White's neck with his left hand.

Blue stops White from attacking by raising his body and using his weight to push down on the back of White's neck. This causes White's head to go down so that he cannot bring his power forward.

White sits up and hooks his right leg around the outside of Blues' left leg, preparing for a sweep or single leg take down.

Blue pushes down on the back of White's head to stop his attacking forward pressure.

Arm Drags.

As is usually the case, the sooner you defend the arm drag, the better. Your opponent is going to want to get to his side, off to your side. You can keep him on his back and in front of you if you commit to reaching back across his head with your free arm, opposite the side he is dragging your arm. You may feel a little unstable as you reach over, but once you get your grip, your stability will return. This technique is very simple and very effective.

Blue is in White's guard. White grabs Blue's arm and sets up an arm drag.

White pulls Blue's right arm across to his right side.

Blue immediately lays his weight on White and reaches his left hand across to the left side of White's neck.

Blue grabs with his thumb inside White's left collar.

Blue posts up on his toes and drives his weight forward into White.

After stabilizing his position, Blue pulls his right arm free. It is important that Blue keep his weight down and driving forward towards White's left side to prevent White from moving toward Blue's back.

Arm Drags

This defense is also very simple and very effective. However, you need to understand that it will only work when your opponent is using a butterfly hook on the same side as the arm that he is dragging. If, after you step to the side, your opponent still insists on dragging your arm, follow up with the previous technique.

White sits up and underhooks Blue's right elbow, preparing for the arm drag.

White pulls Blue's right arm across to his right side. Blue posts his left hand on the mat and steps up with his right foot.

White hooks his left foot under Blue's right knee, setting up the hook sweep.

Blue immediately moves his hips in close to White as he lowers his hips to the mat, preventing the sweep.

Defend attacks by denying your opponent elements he needs to make them work.

Grips to your knees: Undo this grip before trying to pass, it is a setup for a sweep.

- **Pull up:** Hold the bottom of the wrist and pull it up.
- **Pin and kick:** Post your hand on his wrist as you kick back your leg.

Arm wrap: Your forearm is under his armpit. His arm is around yours and holding your lapel.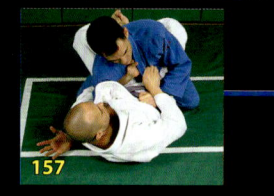

- **Escape:** Move your hand toward his rear, palm up. Pull your elbow toward your head to free your arm.

Guillotine: Avoid this submission with good posture. Once your opponent sinks it in, you will have to use a late defense.

- **Late defense:** Take pressure off your neck by wrapping up his neck and driving weight into his head with your shoulder. Your other arm pulls against the choke.

Collar chokes: Prevent collar chokes by taking the pressure off of your carotid arteries.

- **block the second arm**
- **hide your chin**
- **shield your neck**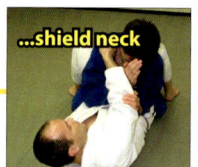
- **push elbows....**  **...shield neck**
- **duck under**

Bow and arrow: The attacker needs a collar grip and his leg over your head.

- **Bow and arrow:** Tear your gi out of his grip. You must be quick and decisive when attempting this late defense.

Arm bars: Defend by denying him the elements needed for the submission to work.

- **Early defense:** As long as your free forearm blocks the inside of his thigh, you should be okay.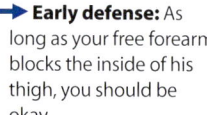
- **Early defense:** Stop him from wrapping his leg over your head by pushing it with your free arm.

▶ **Middle defense:** The hand of the arm being attacked grabs the biceps of the other arm which hand cups behind his thigh.

▶ **Late defense:** Like the technique above accept you are a little bit late so grab around the top of his thigh first, stabilize the position, stack, and then switch you hand to the other

▶ **Late defense:** Smash into him and grab behind his neck to keep him curled up. Now work your trapped elbow free and pass.

▶ **Late defense:** As your opponent goes belly down, throw your legs over his head. Once you are over, the threat is gone.

Omo plata: Your opponent must pin your shoulder to the ground and prevent you from rolling forward to escape.

▶ **Early defense:** Pull your arm straight up before your opponent is able to force your shoulder down.

▶ **Early defense:** Before your shoulder is forced down, posture up and turn your body to uncoil your arm.

▶ **Middle defense:** As your shoulder is forced down, you sense that he is not holding your back. Roll over your trapped shoulder and get on top.

▶ **Your leg is held:** Drive your knee over his chest, donkey kick, jump over.

▶ **Your back is held:** Step your inside leg over his head, sit on his chest, and pull your arm free.

▶ **Late defense:** Post on opposite foot and elbow. Throw the other knee under as you throw yourself under. Pull him over you.

Shoulder lock: Your opponent needs his leg across your waist. You need to stop his leg from crossing your body.

Defense: Push down his foot with your free arm and clear your hips.

Biceps slicer: Your opponent must drive your elbow down near the mat for the move to work properly.

Defense: Lift his knee up to nullify his keylock.

Defense: Lift with your trapped arm and put your knee behing his butt. Use a forearm choke to convince him to abandon the keylock.

Triangle: Keep opponent need to lift his hips and pull down your head to sink the choke.

Early defense: Use posture as a defense. Use your free arm to control his thigh and hips.

Smash defense: Hold on to his gi with your free arm as your other shoulder drives his knee to his head.

Twist defense: Drop on top of the leg that hooks behind your neck. Pull with both hand and rotate your torso into his other leg.

Twist defense: Turn him on his side as you drive forward and circle your lower body.

Knee-in defense: Raise your hips and put your knee on his tailbone. Drop your weight into your kneecap and make good posture.

Late defense: Stand up, hold his sleeves and step on his biceps. As you sit back, twist to pull out your head and arm.

Late defense: Stand up, step over his head, and as you sit back, twist to pull out your head and arm.

Kimura: Your opponent needs to sit up, establish a figure-four grip, and stop you from grabbing anything.

→ **Nullify grip:** Neutralize his grip by climbing over his leg and circling to his back.

→ **From in the guard:** Grab your own gi then push his hip with your free hand and lift your head up.

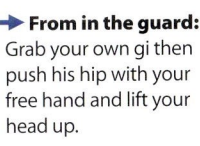   

→ **From in the half-guard:** Grab your trapped arm with your free arm. Drop your shoulder into their and pull up your trapped arm.

Hip bump sweep: Your opponent must get up on his palm or elbow and raise his hips.

→ **block the shoulder**

→ **block the hips**

→ **block the hips**

Lumberjack sweep: Your opponent must wrap your leg and make pressure into the side of your knee.

→ **Pass counter:** Stuff the sweep by dropping your knee into it then swim your arm under and pass.

→ **Step out:** Avoid sweeps by stepping out of them as soon as your opponent tries to control your foot.

→ **Leg attack:** Let your opponent sweep you and as you fall sink in the ankle lock.

 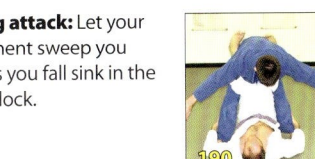  

De la Riva: Your opponent needs a sleeve grip to implement most of his options. Deny him that grip.

▶ **Deny the hook:** Push down the hooking foot, step over it, and go directly to a knee-through-the-middle pass.

▶ **Deny the hook:** Lift up on the heel then smash down the leg with the back of your leg.

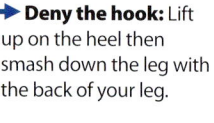    

Sitting guard: Your opponent wants an under-hook, a grip on your elbow, and to sit up.

▶ **Under-hook:** If you have the under-hooks, he doesn't.

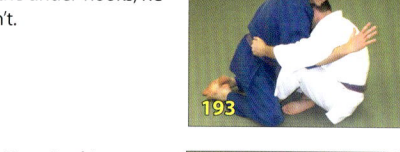

▶ **Flatten:** Put him on his back by pushing under his chin.

▶ **Stuff the head:** Neutralize the position by pushing down on the back of his head.

Arm drag: He wants to pull your arm across his body, exposing your back.

▶ **Cross-grip:** Stop him from going to your back by crossing your free arm to the opposite side of the arm being dragged, then center yourself.

▶ **Pivot:** Circle your lower body and prevent him from getting to your outside.

Chapter 5

Half guard is a position in which you have one leg free and one leg caught between your opponent's legs. The position frequently occurs as you attempt to pass the guard; your opponent will attempt to catch you in the half guard to prevent the full pass. You may also opt to go into your opponent's half guard voluntarily, as the first step in passing a difficult guard. It is important to be aware of the options you have when caught in the half guard and also to be aware of your opponent's options.

When you are in the top position in the half guard, your opponent's first options are usually either to try to sweep you to the bottom position or to put you back in the guard. The sweep will cost you points. Being put back in the guard means you are in greater danger of attack and will have to start your pass all over again. If the fighter on the bottom manages to move around to your back while you are on all fours, it counts the same as a sweep. The opponent also has the option of attempting to apply a knee bar from the bottom.

Being put back in the guard is preferable to being swept; you are still on top and your opponent does not score. You will receive an advantage point for gaining the half guard position, so going into the opponent's half guard and then being put back in the guard results in an advantage for you.

To prevent the sweep or reversal, control your opponent's head and keep your hips low, though there are exceptions, of course. Just like passing the full guard, passing the half guard sometimes requires patience and a methodical approach. In order to pass the half guard and gain side control or the full mount, you must free your trapped leg. There are a number of techniques and variations to free the leg and pass. Most involve maintaining control of the opponent's head/shoulder area and keeping your hips low. It is also important in many of the passes for you to prevent your opponent from controlling your outside (free) knee or hip. Under-hooking the opponent's arm or keeping your hip pressed tightly to the mat will help prevent the opponent from lifting your outside leg or hip. You can also use your free leg to push down on the opponent's legs as you pull your trapped leg free.

There are also a number of submissions that can be set up and completed from the top position in half guard. When on top of your opponent in the half guard, you can attack his far arm with an American lock. You can also choke your opponent with a sleeve choke, and attack with variations of the shoulder lock.

Once you pass the half guard, you should end up in side control or the mount, good positions from which to attack.

Know your options in the half guard as well as your opponent's.

Flattening the Opponent

The first thing to learn about the half guard is the positions that are desirable from the top and the bottom. Get good position on the top, and prevent your opponent from getting a good position on the bottom. Most of the modern strategies from bottom half guard require the player to get on his side and under-hook under the top player's arm on the same side as his trapped leg. So then, as the player passing the guard, you want to keep your opponent on his back and avoid the under-hook on the side of your trapped leg. Getting the under-hook yourself denies it to your opponent. Controlling his head keeps him off his side. The top two techniques are known as the **shoulder of justice**. Use them to control the head. The bottom technique is a simple but effective way to put the opponent on his back, even if he has the under-hook.

Upper Body (Shoulder of Justice)

Blue has his right leg caught in the half guard. Blue's immediate goal is to pin White flat on his back. Blue pins White's left upper arm to the mat so that White cannot turn onto his side.

Keeping his chest down, Blue under-hooks White's head with his left arm.

Blue drives his left shoulder into the left side of White's head for control. Blue simultaneously drives his hips down.

From the third frame above, Blue has good control. By holding the gi and pushing his shoulder into Blue's face, he prevents White from turning or sweeping to White's right, allowing Blue to cheat that way with his base. In this row, Blue makes the hold even tighter, but on the flip side, it ties up both his hands.

Blue under-hooks White's left arm with his left hand.

Blue connects his palms and crushes White with all his weight.

Lower Body

Blue is caught in White's half guard, with White on his right side.

Blue's first goal is to flatten White onto his back. Blue drives forward and stretches his right leg out and back.

Moving his weight to his right, Blue sprawls on top of White. Blue flattens White onto his back.

Flattening the Opponent

Flattening the Opponent (Late)

If your opponent does get on his side with an under-hook, you need to do something immediately. A whizzer grip is a good first step. Thread your arm under his under-hook. Doing so gives you some control over his shoulder. Use that control, along with your body weight and some forward pressure, to put him back on his back.

Blue is caught in White's half guard, with White up on his right side.

As in the spread opposite, Blue is caught in half guard and White is up on his right side.

Blue over-hooks White's left arm for control and lowers his hips.

Blue drives forward into White and grabs around the outside of White's right elbow with his left hand. It is important to grab the arm as close to the ground as possible for maximum leverage.

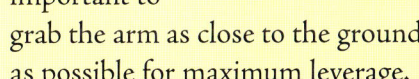

Blue drives forward as he pushes his chest into White's chest.

Blue drives forward and to his right into White as he simultaneously pulls White's supporting right arm out from under him.

Blue drives his hips in and flattens White onto his back.

Blue smashes White onto his back.

206 HALF GUARD ❖ KNEE-FIRST PASS

KNEE-FIRST PASS

This technique requires you to lie to the side of your opponent as you work your leg free. In order to succeed, you cannot let your opponent roll up on top of you. You can prevent that with good grips and positioning. Here, Blue uses a grip over the shoulder to keep White from rolling up onto him. In the next spread, Blue uses a gi trick. Note that Blue could use the grip from the next spread for this technique also.

In this pass and the next, you must get your kneecap out from under your opponent's crossed legs. Until you do, you don't have a chance. Pay close attention to the heel/toe method within the technique. It does not take much energy and will save you a lot of unnecessary struggle.

White catches Blue in the half guard.

Holding under White's left arm with his right hand, Blue reaches over White's head with his left arm.

Blue toes his foot in, moving closer to White's rear; this causes his right knee to push upward. His objective at this point is to get his knee to the other side of White's leg.

Once he gets his knee through, the rest of his leg comes through easily unless White triangles his foot. (Getting a triangled foot free is covered ahead.)

The first three frames of this view give a good depiction of the heel/toe action used to bring up the knee.

Knee-First Pass

Blue pushes off the ball of his right foot and then transfers weight to his heel.

Blue grips White's belt at the rear with his left hand. White's head is behind Blue's left armpit. Then, Blue begins to push down on the inside of White's left knee.

Blue pushes off his heel and brings the ball of his foot toward Blue's rear.

Blue pushes down on White's knee while walking his right foot upward, toward White's rear. Here Blue toes in his foot, pivoting on the heel.

Blue continues moving his foot heel/toe until he gets his knee as high as it will go.

Continuing to push down on White's knee, Blue pivots on the ball of his foot, moving his heel closer to White's rear.

Blue pulls his right knee through White's legs.

Blue reaches underneath White's left arm, twists his hips to the right, and lowers his right knee to the mat.

This is close up of the grips in the mount.

Note how Blue locks his arm out. It takes much less strength to hold things away with the arm straight.

208   HALF GUARD ❖ REVERSE-DIRECTION PASS

REVERSE-DIRECTION PASS

Sometimes with the last technique, you will almost get out of the half guard, but your ankle will get stuck. Some players are tenacious when it comes to keeping your foot between their triangled legs. If you find yourself in that situation, use this technique. For maximum effectiveness, be abrupt when you switch sides.

Blue has already established his grips, positioned his hips, and cleared this kneecap using the technique from the last spread. Blue's right leg is caught in White's half guard. Blue under-hooks White's neck with his left arm and pushes outward on the inside of White's left knee.

Keeping his hips as low as possible, Blue twists his hips to his left, simultaneously under-hooking White's neck with his right arm.

Hugging White's neck tightly, Blue continues twisting his hips to the left, driving his right knee across the top of White's hips. Blue puts his right knee down outside White's right hip.

REVERSE-DIRECTION PASS

Blue posts his left hand on the mat for base and uses the top of his left foot to push back against White's left thigh.

Blue pushes back with his left foot and pulls his right foot free.

Blue establishes the scarf hold position.

210 Half Guard ❖ Lapel-Control Pass

White holds Blue in the half guard. Blue under-hooks White's neck with his left arm, and with the other hand he grabs White's left lapel just above the belt.

Blue pulls the bottom of White's gi out of his belt and feeds it underneath White's left armpit. This grip prevents White from bridging and mounting Blue as he escapes.

Blue feeds the cloth to his left hand with his right hand and grips tightly. This grip is vital, as it will prevent White from rolling on top as the pass continues.

Here is the technique from a different angle after Blue already has the lapel grip established.

Note that even when Blue lifts his hips, he keeps them relatively low.

Lapel-Control Pass

Blue lifts his hips a little and slides his left shin across the top of White's hips.

Blue lowers his left hip to the mat and then Blue lifts his left kneecap and puts it partially across White's belly. Blue pushes his left shin and right hand into White's legs.

Blue pulls his right foot free. Blue is now able to establish side control.

◎ Sometimes a little bit more is needed to get your foot free. Blue gets the extra mechanical advantage he needs by putting his left foot on top of White's right thigh to lever open White's thighs.

HALF GUARD ❖ SLIDING-KNEE PASS

SLIDING-KNEE PASS

If you can get the under-hook with your opponent on his back, consider this technique. Proceed carefully, making sure to keep tight control over your opponent's head as you go.

Blue has his right leg caught in White's half guard. Blue hooks his right arm underneath White's left.

Blue feeds White's collar from his left hand to his right.

Blue pushes White's head to the other side.

Blue now twists his hips to his left and begins to slide his right knee across the top of White's hips.

Blue pushes his right leg through to the mat on White's right side.

Sliding-Knee Pass

Blue lowers his head and presses the back of it against the side of White's face.

Blue posts on the balls of his feet and raises his hips. Blue keeps pressure on White's upper body. Blue reaches back with his left hand and grabs White's right leg.

Blue pushes the leg downward. At the same time, he twists his hips and starts to drive his right knee forward. Blue will drive his leg through forcefully, utilizing gravity and his weight to do so.

Blue pulls his right knee through and pushes White's knee with his left foot. Blue frees his right foot. Blue simultaneously pulls upward on White's right arm to keep White from turning.

Blue scissors his right leg forward and establishes control.

214   HALF GUARD   ❖   INVERTED HALF GUARD

Blue's right leg is trapped in White's half guard. Blue has control of White's head with his left arm.

Blue switches the arm controlling White's head to the right one. Blue grabs the bottom of White's right lapel gi with his left hand.

Blue feeds the gi up and underneath White's right arm. Blue passes the cloth to his right hand, which is underneath White's neck. This traps White's head.

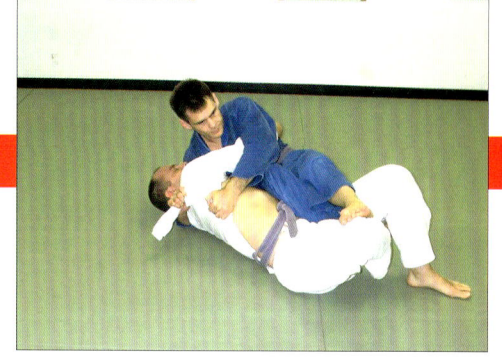

Blue now pushes inside White's right knee and begins to pull his right leg free. Notice that Blue keeps tight control of White's neck with his right hand.

Blue pulls his right leg out as far as possible.

Blue pushes his left foot inside White's right knee so that he can pull his right foot free.

Inverted Half Guard

Blue pushes White's head to his left.

Blue lowers his head to the right side of White's head and posts his left hand for base.

Blue pushes off the mat with his left hand and swings his left leg back to White's left side.

Blue pulls his right foot free and puts the foot on the mat outside White's left hip.

⊙ Blue never releases his grip on White's gi. The hold is crucial so that White cannot roll over on Blue while Blue is positioned to his side.

Blue twists his hips to his right and moves into side control.

216 HALF GUARD ❖ INVERTED HALF GUARD

No one wins all the time, not even Uke. White counters the inverted guard by opening his half guard, quickly inserting his outside (right) hook under Blue's knee (right), and pushing Blue away with it, allowing White to end on top.

INVERTED HALF GUARD

From the inverted half guard, your options and those of your opponent are more limited than from half guard. That has its pros and cons for both combatants, but the top man has the edge if he knows the options. The primary defense to the inverted half guard and two counters to that defense are shown here.

Blue establishes head control with the lapel.

Keeping his upper body weight down, Blue lifts his left leg up and over to his rear.

Blue whips his left leg over to the mat and ends up lying to White's left side.

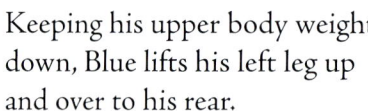

Keeping his upper body weight over White, Blue grabs the top of White's right knee and begins pushing down to free his leg.

White puts his right hook under Blue's right knee as before.

INVERTED HALF GUARD

White begins to lift Blue's right leg for the sweep.

Blue under-hooks White's right knee with his left arm.

White continues to lift Blue's right leg. Blue blocks White's right leg with his left arm as he begins to twist his right knee toward the mat.

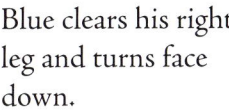

Blue clears his right leg and turns face down.

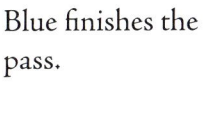

Blue finishes the pass.

Blue is in the same situation in the half guard.

White begins to lift underneath Blue's right knee with his right foot for the sweep.

Blue pushes off his right elbow and lifts his hips up. Blue begins to twist to his right, reaching over White's head.

Blue kicks his left leg over White's legs as he posts his left hand on the mat above White's right shoulder.

Continuing the momentum, Blue drops his left hip and frees his right leg from White's hook, passing the guard.

Trapped Ankle Release

With this technique, once again you need to use the heel/toe technique to walk your foot toward the opponent's butt so that you can clear your kneecap. Clearing your kneecap is key to passing the half guard.

Blue has his left elbow over the top of White's face and the inside of his left arm around White's left shoulder. He is gripping White's belt. Blue uses the heel/toe technique to clear his right kneecap.

Blue under-hooks White's head with his left arm and walks his right foot toward White's hips. At the same time, Blue begins to push the inside of White's left knee outward to loosen the hold on his leg.

Blue pulls his right knee above White's legs and turns face down over White, pushing his knee to the mat.

Blue under-hooks White's left arm with his right arm so that White cannot push Blue's knee. At the same time, Blue hooks the top of his left foot over the top of White's right thigh.

Blue pushes down with his left hook and pulls his right foot free.

Keeping his hips low and hugging White's neck tightly, Blue slides his feet onto the mat, establishing the top mount.

THE LOCKDOWN

THE LOCKDOWN
In the first photo, White has his legs in a figure-four grip around Blue's leg. White's leg position is sometimes called the lockdown. The lockdown can make passing the half guard very difficult if you don't have any answers for it.

From his half guard, White crosses his ankles and hooks under Blue's right foot with his left foot. White straightens his legs for a calf crush.

Keeping his left knee close to White' side, Blue arches his torso upward and pushes down on White's chest with both hands.

> This one is painful for both players, but it is worse for the guy on the bottom.

Blue hooks the top of his right foot over the top of White's left foot, bends his left knee and comes to a standing position.

Blue stretches his left leg back for base, and drives White's feet up close to his rear with his right leg.

Blue brings his left foot back up parallel with his right, and stands up straight. By straightening his right leg, Blue crushes White's left calf against his own right shin.

The Lockdown

Let's look some more at the lockdown. The lockdown is an easy way to slow down a player attempting to pass the guard. It is can be used to set up a number of sweeps and reversals from the bottom, and it sometimes even will cause a submission. You need answers for the lockdown. The previous technique, while effective, is not going to be something you can use all the time, but the techniques here are.

Blue demonstrates the **lockdown** position. Blue hooks the top of his right ankle under White's right ankle. Blue hooks his left leg over the top of White's right leg, then crosses his left foot underneath his own right ankle. Blue extends his legs to apply pressure to White's right calf. The force holds White in place, making it difficult for him to pass the half guard.

White has trapped Blue in the lockdown.

Blue positions his head to the outside of White's hip, to the same side as his trapped right leg. Blue grabs his right wrist with his left hand.

Blue begins to make pressure into the lockdown by using his left shoulder as base to drive his lower body toward White's feet.

In this row of pictures, we get a better view of Blue's legs. Continuing from above, Blue is caught in the lockdown but has already established his grips around White's legs.

Blue stretches his left leg back and drives his hips downward. Blue reaches around the outside of White's left leg with his left arm.

Blue lifts his hips and reaches around the outside of White's right leg with his left arm.

One of the best ways to deal with the lockdown is to avoid it in the first place. Blue does that here by bringing his leg out wide, away from White's feet, then by bringing his heel back close to White's butt where there is not enough space for White to establish control over the leg. Blue's defense has the added benefit of getting his knee up high, in a position where he can clear his kneecap and pass.

Pivot your foot heel/toe to lift your knee.

Having removed all the slack, Blue now proceeds to switch his head to White's right side.

Continuing to squeeze with his arms, Blue posts on the ball of his right foot and pushes with his shoulder as he straightens his right leg. The pressure unwinds the lockdown.

Blue takes advantage of the position and passes White's guard.

Blue grabs his right wrist with his left hand, closing a bear hug around White's upper legs. Blue posts out his left leg and shifts his chest down a bit more toward White's feet.

Blue kicks up strongly with the back of his left leg, breaking the lockdown.

Continuing the momentum, Blue hops over White's legs to his left and passes the half guard.

SUBMISSIONS FROM THE HALF GUARD

The half guard could be considered half way to the mount. That being the case, it should come as no surprise that submissions are possible from it. Generally speaking, being in half guard is better position for submission attempts than being in the guard, but not as good as when you have passed the guard and have the back, the mount, or side control. From top half guard you attack the legs, arms, and head. We will look some attacks in that order.

KNEEBAR

◀▶ White inserts his right leg between Blue's legs to close the half guard.

◀▶ Blue under-hooks White's thigh with one arm and hugs around White's waist with the other.

◀▶ Blue extends his hips and straightens his legs. Blue crosses his ankles below White's ankle and pushes his hips forward, causing pressure against White's knee with his hips. When applying the kneebar, be sure that your hips are above your opponent's knee (never below) and that his knee faces directly into your torso. He pulls with his arms to keep things tight.

Kneebar

Kneebar, far side

White has his right leg between Blue's legs and is about to close his half guard.

Blue quickly under-hooks White's left leg with his right arm, preventing White from locking his legs.

Blue lifts his torso up, twists his hips to his right, and slides his left knee across the top of White's hips. At the same time, Blue begins to slide his right arm toward White's ankle.

Blue slides his left knee under the outside of White's thigh as he lies on the mat beside White. It is important to lie parallel and not perpendicular to the opponent. Blue pinches his thighs together and hugs around White's ankle. Blue now arches his back, pushing his pelvis forward for the kneebar.

American Lock

Blue is caught in half guard. Blue flattens White onto his back and establishes control.

Blue's right hand holds the top of left White's shoulder while Blue's right shoulder pushes White's arm. Blue's left arm switches to the other side of White's head.

Blue smashes White's left arm to the mat with his right shoulder and then grabs the top of White's left wrist with a palm down, no-thumb grip.

Blue under-hooks White's left arm above the elbow and connects his right hand, gripping his left wrist in a no-thumb, figure-four grip.

Keeping his weight down, Blue pulls his left elbow tight into the left side of White's neck. Blue slides the back of White's left hand down the mat toward his hip as he simultaneously lifts White's left elbow upward to complete the American lock.

Kimura

Blue is caught in half guard. White has obtained an underhook under Blue's right arm. Blue reaches his left arm over White's head and posts his elbow on the mat beside White's neck.

Blue slides his right hand along White's arm to the wrist.

Blue grabs White's left wrist with a regular grip.

Driving forward with his body weight, Blue smashes White's left arm to the mat. Blue puts his right elbow against White's left hip and slides his left hand under White's left upper arm. Blue grabs his right wrist with his left hand to make a figure-four grip. Notice the angle of Blue's left arm; it is inserted close to White's left shoulder.

Blue twists to his left and slides White's hand along the mat toward his head as he simultaneously lifts up White's left elbow with his left arm for the Kimura submission.

CHOKES

Use this X-choke variation to when your opponent gets to his side and has the under-hook. If your opponent goes back to his back, beware: if your over-hooking arm is trapped, you could get swept. If you feel that happening, abandon your grips and concentrate on staying on top.

Blue is in half guard. White is up on his right side with an under-hook. Blue over-hooks White's arm with his right arm and grabs White's right lapel with his left hand.

Blue feeds White's right collar to his right hand below White's chin.

Blue now grabs behind White's collar with a left-hand, thumb-in grip.

Blue circles his left elbow around White's head and squeezes his elbows together on either side of White's neck for the X-choke.

Chokes

Ezekiel choke

Use the Ezekiel choke when your opponent is on his back and has, or is looking for, double under-hooks. His neck will be exposed giving you a chance to set in the choke. Make sure that your first arm is in place before you grab the sleeve of the other. You do not want your opponent to have time to defend.

Blue is in half guard. White has an under-hook with his left arm. Blue under-hooks White's head with his left arm.

Keeping his right arm tight to the side of White's left arm, Blue begins to slide the left edge of his hand across the front of White's throat.

Blue grabs inside his right sleeve with the four fingers of his left hand.

Blue pulls his arms to the left as he presses down with the edge of his right hand and lifts his head for the Ezekiel choke.

D'ARCE CHOKE

Look to use the D'Arce choke when your opponent is on his side and does not have the under-hook. That will happen, for instance, if he uses his top arm to try to reach across and grab your ankle to set up a reversal.

Blue is in the half guard with White on his right side.

Blue under-hooks White's left arm with his left hand.

Blue lowers his body and twists to his left as he pulls White's left arm across his left side with an arm drag.

GUILLOTINE CHOKE

Consider this guillotine variation when your opponent get up on his elbow and has an under-hook. It is hard for his to get that position and not open up his neck for attack.

Blue is in the half guard. White has an under-hook with his left arm and is attempting to sit up.

Blue reaches around White's neck with his left arm and grabs his left wrist with his right hand for the arm-in guillotine.

Blue lies down on his left side.

CHOKES

Blue lowers his body over White's left shoulder as he moves his right arm from below White's left armpit past the right side of White's neck. Blue holds the back of White's neck with his right hand to stabilize the position.

Blue presses the back of White's head with his left elbow and grabs his left biceps with his right palm.

Blue bears down with his weight as he squeezes his elbows toward his chest for the choke.

Continuing the momentum, Blue rolls onto his back and locks White's right leg in the half guard.

Blue uses the lockdown to pull White's leg away from his head, which straightens him out, aiding the choke.

Blue arches back, twists to his right, and pulls strongly upward to finish the choke.

⊚ Keep your opponent off his side and on his back when passing the half guard.

position

▸ **The shoulder of justice:** Drive your shoulder into his jaw, forcing him to look away from your free leg. This keeps him off his side and kills reversals.

▸ **Keep him on his back:** Another way to keep him off his side is to circle your lower body.

▸ **Put him on his back:** Cross-face his head and drive him back onto his back.

▸ **Put him on his back:** Keep him off his elbow and side by pulling his elbow to you. Drive your chest into his and put him on his back.

⊚ Get the kneecap of the leg caught in the half guard free before attempting these passes.

passes

▸ **Knee first pass:** Free your knee by moving your foot heel/toe. Keep opponent from rolling into you with a grip over his head and behind his back.

▸ **Reverse-direction pass:** If your foot gets stuck at the end of the knee-first pass, switch grips and then switch your knee to his other side.

▸ **Lapel-control pass:** Use the lapel to keep him off his side while allowing you to wedge your free knee in, while on your side, to open the guard.

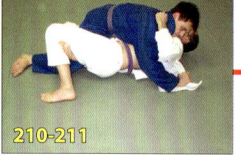 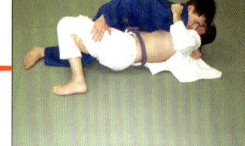  

▸ **Sliding-knee pass:** A lapel grip and your head control him as you lift your hips, push his knee with your free hand, and then slide your knee through.

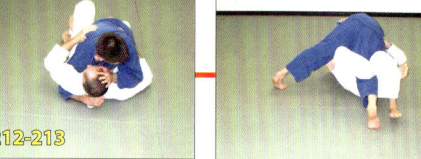  

▸ **Trapped ankle release:** Free the top of your trapped knee then drop it down. Keep your chest tight to his, and use the instep of your other foot to pry your foot free.

◎ **Inverted half guard passes can be attempted without freeing your knee first, but be prepared to counter your opponent's counters.**

▸ **Inverted half guard:** A lapel grip keeps him on his back. Sit on your side and use your free leg to break open the triangle hold he has on your other leg.

214-215

inverted half guard

▸ **Inverted half guard counter:** He hooks his outside instep under your leg, lifts it, and then separates his hips from yours and scrambles to get on top.

▸ **Counter:** Move your hips away and under-hook his outside leg with your free arm. He can no longer scramble to escape.

216-217

▸ **Counter:** As he tries to lift your leg, twist over, putting your weight onto his under-hook, and throw yourself back to his other side.

186-187

◎ **The lockdown presents problems for you as the guard passer. You can turn it into a submission against your opponent, avoid it, or escape it.**

lockdown counters

▸ **Submission counter:** Use his figure-four leg position against him by standing to put a submission on him.

219

▸ **Avoidance:** Avoid the lockdown by hiding your foot near his rear.

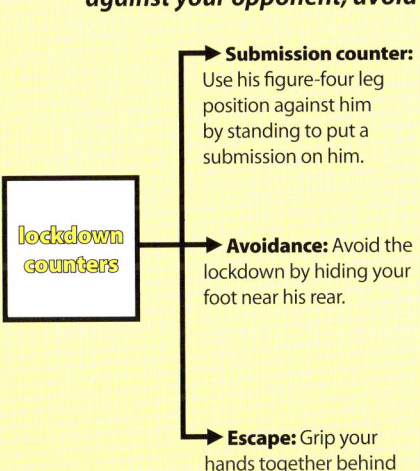 
221

▸ **Escape:** Grip your hands together behind his rear and hug. Lift your hips, post on the ball of your foot, and straighten your leg to create pressure to escape.

220-221

SUBMISSIONS

kneebars

▶ **Kneebar:** Under-hook his outside leg with your arm and cross your legs. Keep your knees close together and use your hips like with an armbar.

▶ **Kneebar:** Attack his other knee. Slide your outside knee over his body, scoop up his leg, cross your arms, and put on the pressure with your hips.

armbars

▶ **Americana:** Make sure both your arms are to the side of his head and that you keep his arm bent.

▶ **Kimura:** Make sure you keep his arm bent as you apply the submission.

> *A variety of submissions are possible from within the half guard. Your chances of successfully applying one increase if your opponent is concerned with you passing his guard.*

chokes

▶ **Collar choke vs. under-hook:** Whizzer your arm in and take a deep grip with one arm. Come over the top, thumb-in with the

▶ **Ezekiel choke:** Another good option for when your opponent has the key under-hook.

▶ **D'Arce choke:** Consider this when opponent is on his side, but does not have an under-hook.

▶ **Guillotine choke:** Consider this if opponent is on his side and has an under-hook.

Chapter 6

ATTACKS FROM INSIDE THE GUARD

Although the dominant strategy while inside an opponent's guard is to pass, there are times when attacking the opponent from inside the guard is advisable. In chapter 3, we saw two choke attacks used primarily to open the legs. This chapter begins with another choking technique and then covers neck cranks. The focus of the chapter, however, is leg attacks.

There are three major types of leg attack from inside the guard: straight foot locks, knee bars and toe holds. There are several variations of the straight foot lock, and it is the most commonly-seen attack from inside the guard. In competition, knee bars and toe holds are usually only allowed at the purple belt level and above.

In order to attack the opponent's legs from the guard, you must first open his legs. That is, you must break the closed guard. Once the opponent's legs are open, the opportunity to attack is created. Successful leg attacks from the guard are primarily dependent on proper timing, as the strength of the legs usually prohibits 'forcing' a technique. The position and movement of the opponent's legs as he works his open guard will determine the types of leg attacks possible.

Foot locks are commonly done by securing the opponent's foot behind your armpit and then falling to the mat, either straight back or to the side. Most straight foot locks are done with the opponent's leg trapped between your legs, so it is important to bring a knee up between the opponent's legs as you fall back. Foot locks can also be done by turning the opponent over onto his face. The opponent's leg position will dictate opportunity. Note that foot locks are difficult to finish if the opponent has a grip on your upper body, as he will be able to ride up as you fall, preventing you from stretching his leg and foot. Knee bars from the guard are of the 'spinning' variety - meaning you need to turn the body 180 degrees to set up the leverage. It is possible to set up the knee bar from between the opponent's legs by spinning outward or from outside the opponent's legs by spinning inward. As for the foot lock, you must trap your opponent's leg between your legs to secure the hold. Unlike the foot lock, the knee bar can be set up from either an over-hook or under-hook grip on the leg.

The toe hold requires you to turn back toward your opponent and secure a figure-four grip around the foot and ankle. The resulting leverage is similar to a foot lock, but the foot is twisted inward as it is stretched. Since the toe hold is usually applied without the opponent's leg trapped between your legs, you must have a good grip on the foot and ankle, with the opponent's foot held tightly to your chest, to apply the hold successfully.

234 Attacks ❖ Ezekiel (Sode-jime)

White hugs Blue's body and pulls him down chest to chest. Blue underhooks White's head with his right arm.

> This technique is an exception to the rule of thumb that you need position before submission. Beware of sweeps when attempting this one as you tend to tie your own hands up. If you have it deep enough, however, it will work from the bottom even after you are swept.

Blue grabs inside his left sleeve with the four fingers of his right hand.

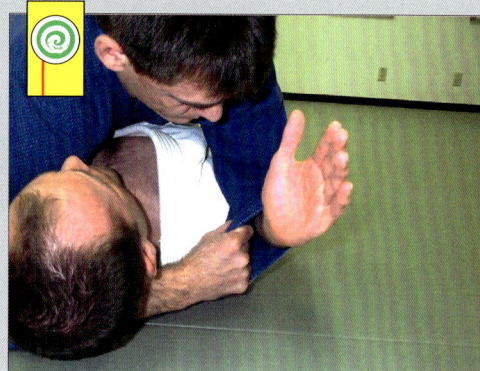

Though it is illegal to grab the end of your opponent's sleeve, it is permissible to grab your own. Here, it is necessary. Grab inside with four fingers for maximum power.

Blue moves his left hand over in a chopping motion on top of White's throat.

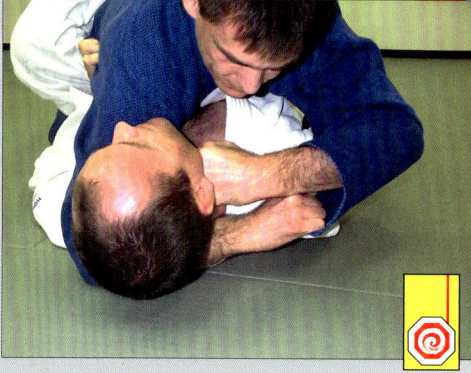

In this variation, Blue uses his fist instead of the edge of his hand.

Blue pulls his left sleeve with his right hand as he presses the knife edge of his left hand down across White's throat for a sleeve choke.

Neck Cranks

White sits up in the open guard.

Blue leans his weight forward, over-hooks White's left arm with his right, and reaches under White's right arm with his left. Sometimes it helps to push the head under the armpit with the opposite arm and then under-hook with the pushing hand (see opposing page).

> Be extra cautious with any submissions involving the spinal column! The potential for serious injury must be taken seriously. It is one thing to hyper extend an elbow and quite another to damage the spine!

Hugging tightly, Blue steps out to his right with his right foot.

Blue moves his left foot across and drops his weight, sitting at White's left side. It is very important to keep hugging tightly and to keep the left elbow locked down so that the opponent cannot pop his head out from under the left armpit.

> Blue puts his palm down on the mat, both for base and to generate leverage to the back of his shoulder.

Blue scissors his left foot through to the front and, hugging tightly with his arms, leans back, applying pressure behind White's head with the back of his left shoulder. White's chin is forced to his chest in a neck crank submission.

This is a variation of the preceding technique. White sits up in his open guard.

Blue pushes on the back of White's head with his right hand, pushing the head under his left armpit.

Blue goes **under** White's left arm in this variation. On the preceding technique he went **over** White's arm.

Blue under-hooks both of White's arms.

Blue steps to the side with his right foot.

Blue scissors his left leg through to the front and leans back for the neck crank.

▲ This is an alternative way to finish the technique. Instead of scissoring the left leg through to the front, you sprawl back both feet and post your palms on the mat. Push up off the mat and arch back for the neck crank submission.

Ankle Locks

◀▶ Blue stands in White's open guard.

◀▶ Blue wraps his right arm tightly around White's right ankle and pushes White's right leg with his other hand.

◀▶ Blue moves his left leg between White's legs and falls back to the mat. As he sits back, Blue pinches his legs together tightly to isolate White's left leg. Blue allows his right arm to slide down White's leg until his wrist is below White's Achilles' tendon, just above the heel.

◀▶ Blue then makes a figure-four lock by grabbing the top of his left wrist with his right hand as he grabs over the top of White's shin with his left hand. Keeping his elbows pulled back and in, Blue lifts his chest and arches his back, pulling up under White's Achilles' tendon and stretching back the top of White's foot for the submission.

238 Attacks ❖ Ankle Locks

White turns to his right side and slides his left shin across Blue's hips in the scissors sweep position.

Blue keeps his hips down and pushes the inside of Blue's right knee with his left palm, pinning White's right leg to the mat. At the same time, Blue begins to wrap White's right ankle with his right arm.

Blue slides his left knee over the top of White's right thigh and falls onto his left side.

Blue locks his hands in a figure-four around White's ankle and begins to bring his left foot over White's left leg.

A basic defense for White would be to grab Blue by the lapels, behind his head, or over his shoulder. That would allow him to pull himself on top of Blue and push his foot through, or put the sole of his foot on the floor. Obviously, then, it is better that Blue keep himself out of reach or that he break White's grip before making his attack.

Blue puts his right foot on the mat, squeezes his legs tightly, and arches his back, while pulling up under White's ankle for the submission.

Using the Feet

Blue sets up the footlock. Blue squeezes White's left leg between his legs and wraps his right arm around Blue's left ankle. Blue pushes White's left hip with his right foot to keep him from sitting up and defending the hold. Blue figure-fours his hands, grabbing his left wrist with his right palm and putting his left palm on top of White's shin.

Blue squeezes his knees together, locks his elbows back tight to his own body, and lifts right wrist upward into White's Achilles' tendon. Blue lifts his chest and arches back. He uses his torso to generate the power for the footlock, not just his arms.

Triangle Leg Control (Banned)

Since the first edition of this book was published, this version of the ankle lock has been banned from many BJJ competitions. This is considered reaping the outside of the knee and apparently that is too dangerous. You cannot wrap your outside leg over and across your opponent's leg from this position. This technique is effective, however, and it is part of the art.

Blue sets up the footlock with a leg scissors hold. Blue crosses his right leg over the top of White's left thigh.

◉ To be good at ankle locks, you need to be good at controlling your opponent with your legs. Putting your feet on his hips or the inside of his thigh generally works.

Here Blue keeps White at a distance by controlling the inside of White's leg with his foot. Note also how Blue has triangled his legs. This is to help make more pressure for the submission.

Blue tightens his grip around White's ankle as he rolls onto his left side and hooks his right foot behind his left knee. Blue's left foot pushes the inside of White's right knee to prevent White from sitting up.

Opposite Hands

In this variation of the above grip, Blue inserts his left wrist under White's left ankle, grabs his right biceps with his left palm and makes a figure-four grip.

Blue arches back and pulls his left wrist up under White's ankle to finish the footlock.

Lapel Grip

Here is an alternate grip for the footlock. Blue inserts his right wrist under White's left ankle and grabs his lapel to lock White's ankle. Blue uses his other hand to pull on his opposite lapel. That keeps the arm locking the foot from slipping along with the lapel.

Knee Bars

White sets up the de la Riva guard with his right foot inserted between Blue's legs from the rear and hooked over the top of Blue's right leg.

Blue turns to his right, pivoting on his left foot and swinging his right foot back a step. As he turns, Blue hooks his right arm under White's right ankle and grabs his left lapel to secure the leg.

Blue sits down as close as possible to White's right hip and wraps his left arm around White's leg.

Blue falls back parallel to White's leg. He simultaneously crosses his ankles and squeezes his legs together tightly.

Hugging White's leg tightly to his chest, Blue arches his back and pushes his hips forward for a kneebar submission.

242 Attacks ❖ Knee Bars

◀▶ Blue is passing White's open guard, and has White's right leg under-hooked with his left arm. Blue holds outside White's left knee with the dual purpose of immobilizing White and providing base for himself.

◀▶ Blue twists his hips and swings his right foot over White's right leg, putting his foot down outside White's right hip. Blue hugs White's leg close to his chest with his left arm.

◀▶ Blue sits straight down on the top of White's right hip.

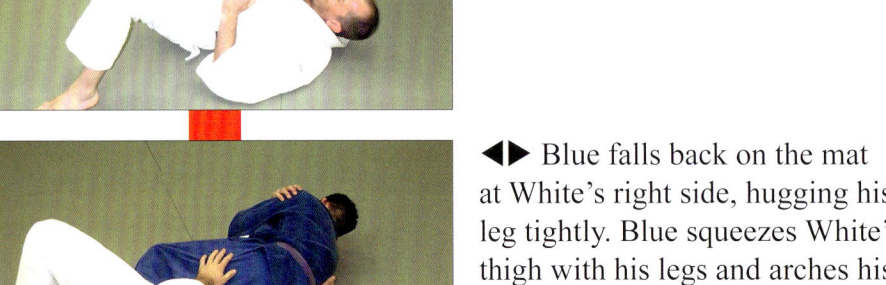

◀▶ Blue falls back on the mat at White's right side, hugging his leg tightly. Blue squeezes White's thigh with his legs and arches his hips for the kneebar.

Knee Bars

Blue is passing White's open guard. Blue wraps his left arm over the top of White's right leg.

Blue slides his right knee through but allows his foot to hook the top of White's thigh. Blue posts with his right hand for base and to aid in the transition to the mat.

Blue lies on the mat, supporting himself on his right elbow. Blue pulls his elbow back as he squeezes his legs and pushes his hips forward for the kneebar. The movement of the hips is similar to a straight-arm armbar.

Blue finishes the move by straightening his body. Everything must be tight before he straightens out.

244 Attacks ❖ Knee Bars

Blue is passing White's open guard.

Blue pivots, pulls up White's right leg and under-hooks White's right ankle with his right arm.

Blue squats and presses his left knee on top of White's right hip.

Blue falls back parallel with White's leg. He squeezes White's right thigh between his legs as he hugs the leg tightly. Blue arches his hips and applies the kneebar.

TOE HOLD

White holds Blue in the de la Riva guard position with his right leg inserted between Blue's legs from the rear and the top of his right foot hooked over the front of Blue's right hip. White grabs Blue's belt with his right hand from the rear. White will pull Blue's belt back with his right hand, attempting to sweep Blue to the rear.

As White pulls back with his right hand and pushes back with his right leg, Blue follows the momentum and turns his body to the right, pivoting on his left foot as he swings his right foot back. Blue hooks his right arm under White's right ankle as he turns.

As always, **BE CAREFUL**. It is easy to hurt someone's knee or pop a tendon in his ankle with this one. With leg attacks, physical damage has a way of happening before the submission is very painful.

Blue grabs the top of White's right foot with his left hand, thumb facing his chest. Blue grabs just below White's toes at the top of his foot. Blue grabs the top of his left wrist with his right hand (his right wrist is wrapped under White's right ankle) in a figure-four position.

Blue lowers his hips, pulls White's right foot toward his chest, and simultaneously pushes down with both hands, twisting White's right foot in an inward spiral for the submission.
This one will lead to knee injuries if the foot is twisted rather than attacking the Achilles' tendon.

◉ There is an argument to be made that this technique violates the prohibition against techniques than twist the knee. For the most part, however, it is allowed in competition between higher belts.

Toe hold

Blue is in the de la Riva guard. White has his left foot wrapped around Blue's right leg.

Blue grabs the top of White's right foot with his left hand, thumb around the big toe knuckle and four fingers wrapped around the little toe knuckle.

Blue reaches over the top of White's ankle and threads his right wrist below White's Achilles' tendon. Blue grabs the top of his left wrist with his right hand in a figure-four grip.

Blue lowers his body and plants his right knee while holding Blue's foot close to his chest.

Blue rolls forward over his right shoulder and hooks below White's left leg with his right leg, knee behind knee.

Stopping on his back, Blue hooks his right ankle behind his left knee and triangles White's left leg tightly. White is pinned on his face. Blue pulls down and in with his right elbow as he simultaneously pushes White's toes toward his rear for the toe hold.

chokes

▶ **Ezekiel:** If your opponent allows you to get your first arm under his head, you can hold the sleeve of the other arm and use the grip as a fulcrum to put on the choke.

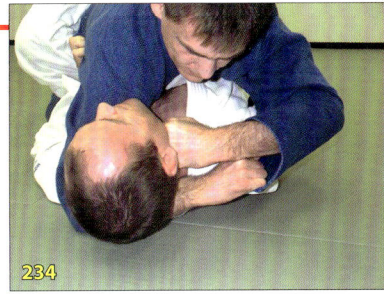

◀ **Ezekiel:** In this variation, you push your fist into his carotid artery instead of the blade of your hand across his throat, as above.

neck cranks

▶ **Neck crank, over-hook:** One arm goes behind his head and in front of his shoulder. Over-hook the other arm and sit to his side.

▶ **Neck crank, under-hook:** Just like above but with an under-hook.

ankle locks

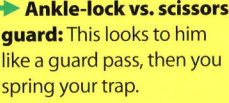

▶ **Straight ankle lock:** Look for this when he leaves his feet dangling to your sides. Make sure to use your legs to control your opponent.

▶ **Ankle-lock vs. scissors guard:** This looks to him like a guard pass, then you spring your trap.

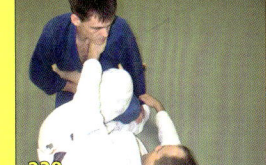  

▶ **Reverse hands:** Sometimes reversing your figure-four grip gives you a better angle to finish.

▶ **Lapel grip:** Instead of a figure-four grip, use your lapel for leverage.

toe holds and knee bars

▶ **Knee bar vs. de la Riva:** If your opponent is not cautious with the de la Riva, attack his knee.

▶ **Knee bar vs. open guard:** The movement and execution are similar to a basic arm bar.

▶ **Knee bar vs. open guard:** In this version, instead of holding the knee with both arms in front of your chest, trap the leg behind your armpit.

▶ **Knee bar vs. open guard:** Attack the knee from the outside.

▶ **Toe hold vs. de la Riva:** Pivot your outside leg, turning your back, and put on the figure-four.

   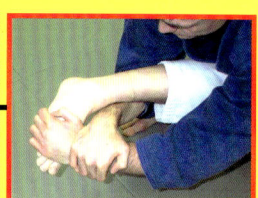

▶ **Toe hold vs. de la Riva, other leg:** He uses a modified de la Riva, you attack his other leg if he puts it on your knee.

Chapter 7

The Turtle Position

The turtle position usually occurs when you are attempting to pass the guard and your opponent back rolls to his knees to prevent you from gaining side control and scoring points. If your opponent back rolls to his knees as you pass, you will have an advantage, but no points will be scored. The danger to the opponent is that he will expose his back to attack, if only momentarily.

As soon as the opponent rolls back to the all-fours position, you need to prevent him from either controlling your legs for a single- or double-leg take-down, or sitting back to his guard. You need to move to maintain your advantageous position. The best way to maintain control of the opponent who rolls back to the turtle position is first to crush him with your weight and then control his head and/or limbs. You may use your chest of one of your hands for this initial control. Without first putting some weight on the opponent's upper back or head, it will be very difficult to control his movement.

Once your opponent rolls into the turtle position, you can control him from a couple different positions as you prepare to attack.

> 1. You can control the opponent from the side position–facing the same way as the opponent with your close knee under the opponent's chest and your outside leg posted on the mat for stability (i.e. pg. 250).

> 2. You can control from the head-to-head position–facing the opponent's feet with your chest pressing down on the back of the opponent's head and upper back (i.e. pg. 271).

In each of these positions, the arms and legs will also be used to control the opponent in various ways: wrist control, hugging the back, locking the head, wrapping the arms, wrapping the legs, etc…. The control position you adopt will dictate the kinds of offensive techniques and submissions that are available to you.

Once you are controlling your opponent in the turtle position, there are a large variety of submissions available. You can attack the opponent's arms, setting up armbars, shoulder locks, and keylocks. You can attack the opponent's neck with chokes and strangles. You can attack the legs as well. In addition to submission techniques, it is also possible to force the opponent into other disadvantageous positions. With the opponent controlled in the turtle position, you can take the back, putting your hooks in for points as you set up submission techniques. You can break the opponent down flat on his stomach and then attack. You can also turn the opponent onto his back, coming into the side control position.

Most of the techniques shown in this chapter begin with the opponent to the side rather than head-to-head. It is relatively easy to rotate from a head-to-head position to a side-by-side position. It is also relatively easy to switch from one side to the other. Whatever the transition, be mindful to keep some weight on your opponent. Most attacks from the head-to-head situation are chokes. Look for openings for a choke whenever in this position. If there are none, move to the side.

Take advantage of the turtle position when your opponent gives it. It is a bad position for him. As the chapter illustrates, there are many opportunities for the player on top to attack.

White is in the turtle position. Blue kneels at White's right side and holds over White's back with his left arm. Blue reaches underneath White's chest with his right arm, grabbing around the outside of White's left upper arm.

This variation starts from the same position. Blue reaches underneath White's chest and grabs around his left upper arm with his right hand.

Blue reaches his left arm in front of White's right thigh, and reaches under White to grab his left ankle.

Blue reaches his left arm underneath White's chest and grabs around the other side of White's left upper arm.

Blue lifts his knees and pushes off the balls of his feet while pulling with his hands. The pressure rolls White onto his back (Blue's grips prevents White from posting his left arm or leg to stop the movement).

Blue lifts his knees and drives forward off the balls of his feet as he pulls in on White's left arm.

The position from another angle.

Blue brings his knees up and establishes side control.

Blue rolls White onto his back.

ARMLOCKS

TURTLE ARMLOCKS

If you can scoop your opponent's arm under your front leg, there are ways to submit him if he leaves it straight (below), turns if forward (right), or turns it back (next spread).

White goes to the turtle position. Blue drives his left knee underneath White's chest. Blue holds the back of White's collar with his right hand and the back of White's belt with his left hand. Blue keeps his weight pressing down on White's back.

White steps his right foot over White's right forearm and slides the arm out.

Blue pulls White's right arm back straight with his right leg.

Blue crosses his ankles underneath White's wrist, straightens his legs, and presses down with his hips for an armbar. It is important to trap the opponent's arm with the back of the elbow facing upward.

From the previous technique, White counters the armbar by bending his elbow and moving his hand upward.

Blue changes his base by twisting his hips forward as he reaches over White's back with his left arm. Blue slides his left knee on the mat close to White's side.

Blue scissors his left knee underneath White. He sits on his hip and twists back, cranking White's right arm. The submission is an American lock variation.

252 THE TURTLE POSITION ◆ ARMLOCKS

TURTLE ARMLOCKS

On this spread, there are two options for when your opponent turns his hand back and palm up to avoid the armbar from the last page. Both techniques are Kimura variations applied with the legs. The first option is simple. It works well against beginners, but against experienced opponents you may have a tough time getting the tap and/or maintaining your base. The second option is more difficult to execute, but the finishing position is more stable. Even if your opponent does get out of it, you will be in side control.

Continuing from the last page, this time White twists his right arm back to avoid the straight armbar.

Blue bends his left leg back to trap the arm and twists his hips so his right thigh slides under White's shoulder. Be sure to keep your hips over the back of the opponent's shoulders with the weight down so the opponent cannot roll forward. The result is a chicken-wing-type shoulder lock.

Blue establishes the knee-under-belly position in preparation to attacking White's turtle position. Blue has his left knee under White's belly and his left arm wrapped over White's back. Blue establishes wrist control on White's left wrist with his left hand. Blue pushes off his right foot and smashes down on White's back.

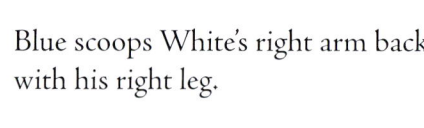

Blue steps his left foot over the top of White's right arm.

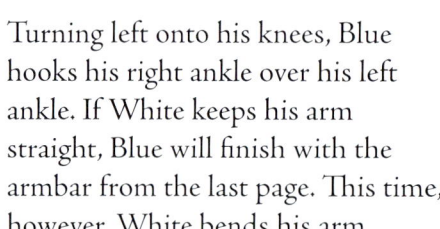

Blue scoops White's right arm back with his right leg.

Turning left onto his knees, Blue hooks his right ankle over his left ankle. If White keeps his arm straight, Blue will finish with the armbar from the last page. This time, however, White bends his arm.

Blue senses that White's arm is twisting and moves White's right wrist over the back of his left ankle. He does so by lifting it up with his right leg while sliding his left ankle under. White's right wrist is stuck on top of Blue's left ankle.

ARMLOCKS

Blue turns back to his right and lowers his weight. Blue posts his right hand out wide for base.

Blue moves his left arm across the front of White's right shoulder and under his left armpit.

Turning his head to his right, Blue rolls over his left shoulder.

As Blue rolls up, he pulls White over with him, with his left leg pressuring behind White's right arm.

Blue comes up from the roll as White tumbles over onto his back.

Blue sits up, bends his left leg back, and lifts his hips off the mat. Blue pulls back with his left leg as he drives his hips forward for a chicken-wing submission. Note that Blue's left arm is still extended over White's head to keep White pinned to the mat.

TRIANGLE

If you can get your knee in under your opponent's chest and behind his triceps, not only can you scoop that arm with your legs, you can also hit a reverse triangle choke. Sometimes it is tough to get the right angle to finish with a reverse triangle. If that is the case, use the hold for control and attack the opponent's free arm.

Blue establishes the knee-under-belly position on White's left side.

Blue reaches under White's right armpit with his right hand as he slides his right knee forward under White's left armpit.

Blue steps over White's head with his left foot.

Blue hooks the back of his left leg tightly around the back of Blue's neck.

Triangle

Blue locks his hands together under White's right armpit.

Pushing off with his left foot, Blue falls backward and slides his right knee under White's left armpit. Blue simultaneously pulls White's right arm back as he falls.

Blue straightens his right leg and begins looping it over White's left arm.

Blue locks his left ankle behind his right knee. Blue squeezes the triangle choke as he pulls White's right arm toward his chest for the submission.

The Turtle Position ❖ Clock Choke (Koshi-jime)

White back rolls out of the guard and goes to his hands and knees in the turtle position. Blue grabs four fingers inside White's rear collar with his left hand and holds the back of White's belt with his right hand. Blue presses his right knee in between White's left elbow and knee and posts his left foot out for base.

Blue lifts up on White to make space to slide his right knee under White's chest and then Blue drops his weight onto White's back.

Blue reaches his right hand under White's right armpit and grabs White's right collar with his right hand.

Clock choke
The clock choke is the bread-and-butter submission against the turtle position. Once you get a deep grip, it is deadly and hard to defend. Getting the grip is typically the hardest part. Once you get it, though, you have multiple ways to finish your opponent. The key to finishing the standard clock choke (above and below) is hip placement. Make sure to move your hips over your opponent's shoulder and then sit down on it as you finish the move.

In this variation, instead of grabbing White's wrist with his right hand, Blue grabs White's left lapel for control. This increases the action of the choke but decreases Blue's control of White.

Blue scissors his right leg through to the front.

Blue thrusts his hips forward and pulls his left elbow back to complete the choke.

Clock Choke (Koshi-Jime)

Reaching above White's left arm, Blue slides his left wrist across the front of White's throat and grabs inside White's right collar with a thumb-in grip as far behind the neck as possible.

Blue now lets go of White's lapel with his right hand and grabs White's right wrist for wrist control.

Blue scissors his left foot through to the front and moves around the front of White's head while pulling his left elbow back to finish White with the clock choke. Blue sits his weight onto White's shoulder and pulls the opposite direction. Note how Blue lifts his shoulder.

In this variation of the clock choke, Blue obtains the cross collar grips.

Blue lowers his left knee and shoulder toward the mat.

Blue posts his head on the mat and pulls outward strongly with both hands for the submission.

Feeding the Gi

Use one hand to make it easy for the other to get a deep grip. The idea is to make space for an easy entry. Feeding the gi from one hand to another is key to many techniques.

Blue feeds White's left collar to his right hand (the right arm must be above White's right arm).

Blue pulls the slack out of the cloth with his left hand and grabs as far up the collar with his right hand as he can.

Clock choke variations

If, for whatever reason, the clock choke fails, consider whether you have a good, deep, collar grip in place. If you do, consider putting the grip to use with another choke variation.

Blue attempts to set up the clock choke, grabbing inside White's lapel with his right hand. White pulls down on Blue's arm and blocks the grip of the second hand.

Maintaining his grip on the collar, Blue stands and pushes down on the back of White's head with his left hand, preventing White from escaping the position.

Blue steps his right leg over the top of White's head.

If he tackles your leg...

Blue attempts the above technique, but White grabs around his right leg for a single-leg take down.

The position from a different angle.

Blue grabs White's belt with his left hand.

Clock Choke Variations

Blue twists a bit to make things tighter.

Blue pulls upward with his right hand so that his wrist bone cuts into the right side of White's neck as he simultaneously straightens his right leg, squeezing his calf into the left side of White's neck for the strangle.

⊚ Variation: Blue slides his right shin across the back of Blue's neck behind his right arm. Blue then pushes down with his shin and pulls up with his right arm for the strangle.

Blue presses his left shin behind White's left shoulder.

Blue falls back and extends his right leg straight over the back of White's head, hooking his foot underneath White's left armpit.

Controlling Blue with his right leg and left grip, Blue pulls with his right arm and pushes with the back of his leg for the choke.

Spinning clock choke

This is a tricky way to finish with the clock choke grip. The downside to this approach is that as you step over, you open up space for your opponent to escape. The upside is the element of surprise and a powerful finish.

Blue has White in the knee-under-belly position. Blue reaches under White's throat with his right hand.

Blue grabs inside White's left collar with a thumb-in grip.

Blue posts his left hand on the mat above White's left shoulder and swings his left leg over White's back.

Blue sits on White's back and continues spinning to his right.

Blue brings his left leg over the back of White's neck.

Blue sits down at White's left side. Blue pushes away with his legs as he pulls with his right hand for the choke.

Reverse Grip

If you have your grip reversed...

This is not a clock choke. This is a technique for when you are to your opponent's side and he is in the turtle position, as for the clock choke, but you are gripping the opposite lapel and your forearm is to the other side of his head. This is a good one to have up your sleeve if your opponent manages to free his arm as you roll to the crucifix position (next spread). It is also a good option if you just want to move to side control instead of fighting against the turtle position. Here we show Blue finishing with the choke. It is easy to imagine how he might transition to side control from the choke.

Blue kneels at White's right side and reaches over White's head with his right arm. Blue grabs inside White's right collar with four fingers inside the cloth.

Blue steps his right leg over White's head.

Blue moves his weight forward and posts his weight on his right foot.

Blue swings his left leg over White's back.

Blue sits down at White's right side.

Blue pushes away with his legs as he pulls back with his right hand for the choke.

Follow-up

If the opponent turns into the choke to defend, he will do so at the expense of exposing his arm. Your legs are already position for the juji-gatame, so scoop under his arm and finish him with it.

From either of the two previous techniques, Blue loses the grip on the collar as he sits back to choke.

Blue under-hooks White's left arm with his left hand.

Blue secures White's left wrist, squeezes his knees, and lifts his hips for the arm bar.

FOLLOW-UP: ROLLING CHOKE

This is a good one to have up your sleeve if your opponent manages to free his arm as you roll to the crucifix position (next spread). It is also a good option if you just want to move to side control instead of fighting against the turtle position. Here we show Blue finishing with a choke. It is easy to imagine how he might transition to side control from the choke.

Blue sets up the clock choke. Blue has a right grip, thumb in, inside White's left collar. Blue reaches underneath White's left arm with his left.

Blue does a forward roll over White's left shoulder.

The roll flips White over onto his back.

White bridges on top of Blue.

White back rolls over Blue, attempting to escape the choke.

Blue maintains his grips and rolls up with White.

FOLLOW-UP: VS. BACK-ROLL ESCAPE

From the technique above, or from the crucifix (next spread), sometimes your opponent will try to escape with a back roll. If that happens, keep your grips and go with them. You will end back at the starting position for the clock choke. In addition to your clock choke attacks, from there you can attack his arm by scooping it up with your leg as we saw earlier, or roll to the crucifix, as we will see next.

Clock Choke Follow-Ups

Blue slides his hips away from White's head, while maintaining his grips.

Blue scissors his left leg back under his right. Blue pushes his right shoulder into the back of White's head as he scissors his legs so that White does not escape.

Blue turns to his belly while at the same time pulling with his right arm, increasing the pressure of the choke. It is important to maintain the grip around the opponent's left arm with your left arm so that he cannot turn out of the choke. Blue uses his shoulder to make pressure also.

Blue comes up on his knees and drives his left knee underneath White.

Blue is in position to submit White with the basic clock choke or top scoop up White's arm with his leg.

264 THE TURTLE POSITION ❖ CRUCIFIX ENTRY

CRUCIFIX ROLL

If you can get to the crucifix position, you will have your opponent on the defense and in trouble. Controlling his arm with your legs is key, and if you do not have it, you are likely to wind up on the bottom in his side control. So get it, preferably before you commit to the roll. All the entries in this book show the entry with a deep collar grip. You can also enter without a collar grip if you control over his other arm with your arms. Either way works, but we like the collar grip because the choke is already in place, and escape is more difficult.

Blue traps White's arm between his legs as in the techniques on pgs. 251-253. Blue grabs underneath White's neck with his right arm, and reaches over White's back with his left arm.

▲▼Blue grabs inside White's left collar with his right hand, thumb in. Blue then under-hooks White's left arm with his left and secures the grip by grabbing his own right lapel.

Blue turns his head to his right and rolls over White's back, turning White face up.

In the technique above, Blue already has White's right arm trapped. Below is one way Blue might trap White's arm. Note that unlike the armlock techniques on pgs. 251-253, here it does not matter which way White turns his trapped arm; it is still trapped well enough for the crucifix roll however he turns it.

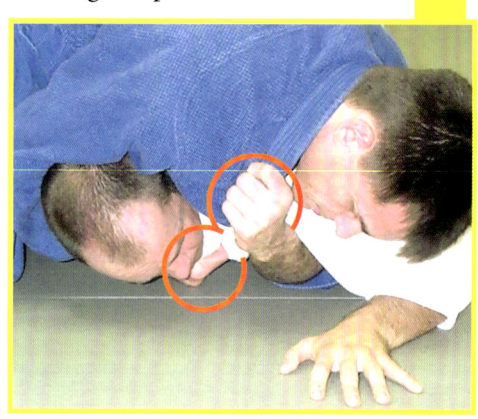

With White in the turtle position, Blue drives his left knee underneath White's chest. At the same time, Blue hugs White's back with his left arm and controls White's right shoulder with his right grip.

Blue twists his hips to his right and uses his left knee to slide White's right arm away from his body.

Blue quickly steps his right foot over the top of White's right arm and hooks the wrist.

CRUCIFIX ENTRY

265

Blue holds White in the crucifix position. Blue controls White's left arm with his left arm and pulls with his right arm to choke White.

In this variation, Blue slides his left hand behind his head instead of holding his lapel as in the other photo sequences on this spread. Putting his hand behind his head stretches out White's left arm more, making it harder for White to defend.

Blue scissors White's right arm and inserts his left hand below White's left arm for wrist control.

Blue pushes off the mat with his left foot and rolls over White's back, turning White face-up in the crucifix position. Blue grabs his own lapel with his left hand to secure White's left arm.

Blue pulls with his right arm to choke White. Blue's left hand releases White's wrist and switches to help apply pressure to White's neck to finish the choke.

CRUCIFIX FINISHES

Blue takes wrist control with his left hand and slides his right shin behind White's neck. Blue then pushes forward with his right shin and pulls with his left arm to complete the choke. You may need to make a small snake (hip) movement to make space to get your leg behind the neck.

Blue has completed the roll and holds White in the crucifix position. Blue now has many options for submitting White.

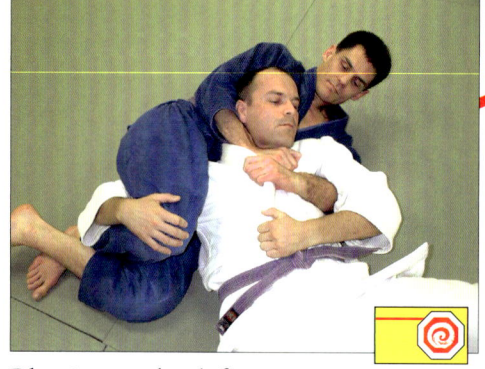

Blue inserts his left arm beneath White's left arm and grabs White's right lapel. Blue then pulls back with his right arm as he pushes down with his left hand to complete the choke.

Blue reaches below White's left armpit and holds his lapel.

Blue then slides his left hand down behind White's neck in a chopping motion (leading with the little finger) as he simultaneously pulls back with his right arm to finish the choke.

CRUCIFIX

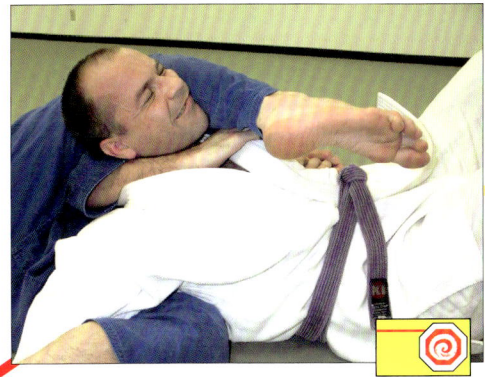

Blue maintains the grip on White's left collar with his right hand. Blue then brings his right leg up and over White's head and hooks the back of his right knee on the left side of White's head. Blue pulls back with his right leg and simultaneously pulls with his right arm to finish the choke.

The choke from another angle.

Blue keeps his right leg hooked tightly around White's right arm and reaches his right arm over the top of White's left arm.

Keeping his hips low behind White's neck, Blue twists his body to the left, forcing White's chin to his chest for a neck crank (This is illegal in most competitions).

Blue grabs his own lapel with his left arm to secure White's left arm.

Blue arches his body and pushes down with his legs to stretch out White's right arm for shoulder and elbow pressure.

Belt-grab armbar

White is in the turtle position. Blue sprawls on the back of his head. Blue holds inside White's belt at the rear center with his left hand palm up. Blue uses the belt as a fulcrum and pushes down on White's back with his left elbow to hold White down. Blue is also holding the back of White's collar with his right hand for control.

Blue inserts his right arm under White's left arm while keeping his weight down.

Keeping his grip on the belt, Blue grabs his left wrist with his right, figure-four style.

It is difficult to initiate the entry to the techniques on this spread and the next page against experienced opponents, because they tend to keep their elbows in tight to their bodies from the turtle. Opportunities do arise, however, and chance favors the prepared. If you can lock in your figure-four grip under your opponent's arm, consider attacking it with the methods shown.

Armbar dropping forward

Blue holds White in the same position as above.

Blue under-hooks White's left arm with his right arm and grabs his own left wrist.

Blue brings his knees up and sits on the back of White's head.

Belt-Grab Attacks

269

Blue brings his knees up and sits on the back of White's head, pinching White's head between his knees.

The position from the opposite side.

Blue begins to twist to his left, driving his left knee into White's side as he pulls up on White's left arm.

Blue falls back, trapping White's head below his right leg as he brings his left knee up behind White's left armpit.

Blue finishes with an armbar

Blue now grabs his own left lapel with his right hand, locking White's left arm to his chest. Blue posts his left palm on the mat for base and turns to his right.

Blue continues turning to his right as he slides his left knee over White's back. Blue lowers his left hip to the mat and slides his left knee underneath White's left arm. Blue's right shin pushes against the left side of White's head.

Blue pinches his knees and pushes his legs forward as he arches his back, pulling White's left arm straight into an armbar.

270 THE TURTLE POSITION ❖ BELT GRAB ATTACKS

KEY LOCK

Whereas most experienced opponents are likely to sense what you are up to with the techniques on the last spread, this one will catch most off guard, at least once. The trick is to enter like you intend to go for the previous techniques but then abruptly change directions. You spin the opposite way for this one, and your opponent should be fooled. As with any key lock, you need to get your bones positioned deep behind his elbow (or knee, as the case may be) from the beginning in order for it to be effective.

White is in the turtle position. Blue sits over the back of White's head and grabs the back of White's belt with his left hand for control. Blue begins to reach under White's left arm with his right hand.

Blue turns his body to the left and inserts his right arm through White's left armpit.

Blue falls to his back at White's left side. Blue maintains his grip on the back of White's belt with his left hand and grabs his own left wrist with his right hand.

Blue holds down White's head with his left leg and begins to move his right leg over the top of White's right arm.

Blue locks his feet and squeezes his knees around White's left arm.

Blue grabs his left biceps with his right hand, turning his wrist so the wrist bones press into White's biceps and forearm. Blue extends his legs and simultaneously pulls his left wrist toward himself for a key lock on White's left elbow.

Gator Roll

The next three techniques all involve rolling yourself under your opponent to roll him over you. The technique for the roll is similar in each case, but the finishes vary. Learn the next three techniques together so you can put them together to maximize their effectiveness. This first technique, the gator roll, works great with or without the gi and has proven its effectiveness in mixed martial arts competitions.

Blue sprawls over White's head. Blue wraps his right arm around White's head and inserts his right hand behind White's right armpit.

Blue uses his right hand to push White's right elbow underneath his chest.

Blue extends his right hand as far past White's armpit as possible. Blue now grabs his left biceps with his right hand.

Blue grabs over White's back with his left hand and begins to lower his head to White's right side.

Blue rolls onto his left side and inserts his head under White's right armpit. The torque causes White to fall onto his right side.

Continuing the roll, Blue rolls across his back onto his right side.

When Blue is fully on his right side, he stops the roll.

Blue simultaneously squeezes his elbows in toward his chest as he pushes his hips into the back of White's head. The pressure of Blue's hips forces White's chin toward his chest as Blue's arms tighten around White's neck for the submission.

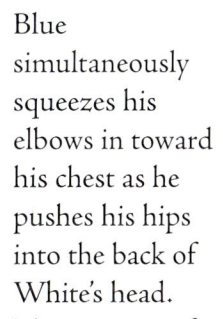

272 THE TURTLE POSITION ❖ ROLLING CHOKES

ROLLING COLLAR CHOKE

With the gi you can use a collar grip to finish the choke. The initial roll is like the gator roll, but the finish is different.

White is in the turtle position. Blue lays across White's shoulders and holds over his back with his left arm. Blue grabs White's right lapel with his left hand and feeds the collar to his right hand. Blue reaches his right hand underneath White's neck.

Blue grabs inside White's right lapel with his right hand, four fingers inside the lapel.

Blue grabs White's right elbow with his left hand.

Here is another view of the technique. You get a better sense of the lateral movement involved from these photos. Note how Blue's head ducks under as he rolls White over. You do not want to pull your opponent down on top of your head. Dive your head under to avoid that unpleasant result.

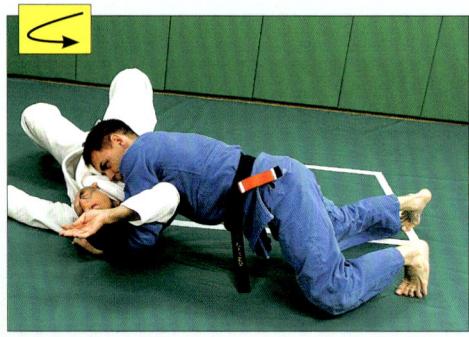

ROLLING CHOKES

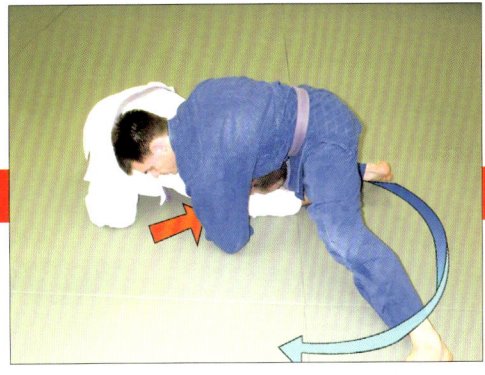

Blue pulls White's right arm back under White's head to break his base. Blue simultaneously moves his hips around the top of White's head; he shuffles his feet to his left.

Blue twists to his right, laying his left side on the mat as he ducks his head underneath White's right armpit. He scissors his legs as he rolls.

Blue continues to roll to his right, pulling White over his chest.

With White flat on his back and Blue's head clear, Blue scissors his feet.

Blue continues to turn until he is face down. Blue slides his left arm behind White's head for control and pulls with his right to finish the choke.

This variation is not, in our experience, as effective as the finish above. It does work, however, and some may prefer it.

After the roll, Blue can also secure White's right arm by gripping behind his shoulder.

Blue twists face down and pulls with his right hand to finish the choke.

Gator Roll to Mount

On this spread are two variations on getting to the mount from attacking the turtle, first with the gator roll and then with a collar grip. The technique on this page uses the same figure-four grip as the gator roll on pg. 271 and can be used in combination with it, particularly if the opponent prevents you from completing the roll part of the gator roll by basing his feet wide as you both are on your backs.

Blue sprawls over White's head. His chest weighs down White.

Blue feels he cannot complete the roll to finish the choke as in the previous technique. Blue immediately back rolls over his right shoulder.

Blue wraps his right arm around White's head and inserts his right hand behind White's right armpit.

Blue spreads his legs open and lands in the top mount as he comes over the top.

Blue extends his right hand as far past White's armpit as possible. Blue now grabs his left biceps with his right hand.

Blue uses his heels to pull himself into the mount.

Blue rolls onto his left side and inserts his head under White's right armpit. The torque causes White to roll over his right side onto his back.

Blue fixes his base and establishes the mount.

Rolling Attacks

With a secure grip (*see below*), Blue sprawls back and puts weight over the back of White's head.

Blue begins to twist his right side down to the mat.

Blue lies on his right side, scissors his right leg through, and begins to duck his head underneath White's left armpit.

Blue continues to roll over to his left side, rolling White over his head while turning White onto his back.

Once White is on his back and Blue's head is clear, Blue begins to back-roll over on top of White. Blue rolls over his shoulder, not his head.

▲▼Blue lands in the top mount position. Blue now twists his body to the right and pulls with his right hand for a choke.

FIGURE-FOUR ROLL TO MOUNT

This technique is similar to the one on the last page, but the grips are different. On the last page, Blue's right arm went under White's head, then out behind White's right armpit, where Blue connected it with his left arm. Here, Blue's right arm goes under White's other (left) armpit first, then to a lapel grip on the other side of White's head. In both cases, the rest is basically the same, with Blue rolling White over the shoulder he has trapped. The grip here dovetails nicely with the chokes on the next spread.

Close-up of the grip: Blue is over White's head. Blue grabs White's right lapel with his left hand, thumb in, and reaches underneath White's left arm with his right hand.

Blue feeds White's left collar to his right hand, gripping with four fingers inside the lapel.

Blue now grabs his own right wrist with his left hand.

276 THE TURTLE POSITION ❖ BREADCUTTER

BREADCUTTER ROLL

On this spread, there are several breadcutter-type chokes. The first two rely on the gi; the second two do not. With the first three, Blue brings in his bottom (right) arm under White's left armpit. Many opponents do not worry too much about this grip because they believe their neck is safe as long as their arm is in the way. Obviously, that is not the case.

Blue holds inside White's right lapel with his left hand while keeping his weight sprawled on White's upper back.

Blue reaches underneath White's left armpit with his right hand and grabs inside White's right collar with a four-finger grip.

Blue now grabs the back of White's collar with his left hand, thumb in.

The hold from a different angle.

Blue lowers his left elbow toward the mat and moves his feet back.

Blue scissors his left leg across and below his right leg and lies on his left side right next to White's left leg, as close as possible.

Blue twists toward his right, pulling White over the top of his chest.

White lands on his back at Blue's right side.

Blue continues turning to his right and comes to his knees. Blue pulls with his right hand as he simultaneously pushes his left elbow downward to finish the choke.

BREADCUTTER

BREADCUTTER

This technique is a variation on the one from the preceding page. Here, instead of going on his back, Blue is able to set the choke by focusing his weight into his forearm and keeping it there. The action of Blue's leg stepping under and through is similar for both techniques.

After Blue has his right grip in place (Blue reaches behind White's left arm and grabs four fingers inside White's right lapel), he grabs the back of White's collar with his left hand, thumb in.

Blue twists his hips to the right and drops his left hip toward the mat as he pulls with his right hand and pushes his left elbow downward for the choke.

Blue reaches under White's throat with his right arm. The radial wrist bone is against White's throat with the palm facing outward.

Blue places the bottom of his left forearm on the back of White's neck. Blue locks his palms together with the right thumb on top of the left. Blue squeezes his elbows together for the choke.

Blue inserts his right arm from behind White's left armpit until his radial wrist bone is under White's throat.

Blue places the bottom of his left forearm on the back of White's neck. Blue locks his palms together with the right thumb on top of the left, closing the three-quarter nelson hold.

Blue drops his weight on the back of White's head and begins to push down on the back of White's neck with his left forearm.

BREADCUTTER TO D'ARCE

If the last variation of the breadcutter does not cause your opponent to tap, use it to set up the D'Arce choke.

Blue twists his arms, torquing White's head counterclockwise.

The torque causes White to fall onto his right side. Blue pulls in on the back of White's head with his left hand.

Pressing his weight down on White's back, Blue inserts his right hand as far as possible past the back of White's neck.

Blue grabs his left biceps with his right hand.

Blue reaches up as far as possible with his left hand and places the hand on White's back. Blue lowers his left elbow to the mat and, dropping all his weight on White's back, pulls in with his elbows for the choke.

GUILLOTINES

ARM-IN GUILLOTINE

If Blue obtains the arm-in guillotine position and manages to pull White's upper body upward as he hops to the squat position, Blue will slide into the half guard position under White and finish the arm-in guillotine.

Blue sprawls over White's head at a 45-degree angle. Blue inserts his right arm behind White's left arm and across White's throat.

PERUVIAN NECKTIE

If Blue obtains the arm-in guillotine position and after hopping up cannot lift White's upper body to make space to slide under White for the regular arm-in guillotine, Blue will opt to sit over White's head for the Peruvian necktie.

Blue sprawls over White's head at a 45-degree angle. Blue inserts his right arm behind White's left arm and across White's throat.

Blue grabs his right wrist with his left hand and hops up onto his feet, close to White's head.

Blue grabs his right wrist with his left hand.

Blue pulls up on White' neck, lifting White's head upward.

Blue hops into the squatting position over White's head. Note how Blue steps his left leg completely over the top of the White's head so that the back of Blue's left leg presses the back of White's neck.

Blue squats under White and begins to sit back.

Blue sits down close to White.

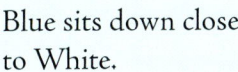

Blue slides his left leg between White's legs and locks White's left leg in the half guard. Blue simultaneously arches back and twists to his right to choke White.

As Blue sits on the mat, he swings his right leg over White's back. Blue now pushes away with his legs as he pulls in with his arms to choke White.

GUILLOTINE:

If Blue obtains the regular guillotine grip around White's neck, he will opt to pull White in for the standard guillotine choke.

Blue sprawls over the top of White's head.

Blue wraps his right arm around Blue's neck so that his radial wrist bone is across White's throat. Blue grabs the little finger side of his right palm/wrist to secure the hold.

Keeping his upper body weight pressing down and his hold tight, Blue steps his right foot forward onto the mat.

Sliding his left foot forward from below his rear, Blue sits back onto the mat.

Blue hooks his right calf over the top of White's left calf and puts his left hook inside White's right hip to stop White from passing around Blue's legs. Blue arches back, squeezes his elbows together, and pulls his right wrist into White's throat for the submission.

Guillotines

Ten-finger choke

If Blue is unable to wrap his arm all the way around White's neck for the guillotine, Blue will opt for the ten-finger choke. Unlike the rest of the chokes in this chapter, the ten-finger choke puts pressure on the throat rather than cutting off blood to the carotid arteries.

Blue sprawls over White's head.

Blue wraps White's head with his right arm and hooks the base of his thumb below White's throat.

Blue curves the fingers of his right hand.

Blue grabs under the little finger side of his right hand with the four fingers of his left hand.

Blue grabs around the little finger side of his right hand with the four fingers of his left hand.

Blue lifts his upper body upward and simultaneously pulls upward with his hands to finish the choke.

Blue pulls upward with both hands.

Taking the Back

There are many strategies and techniques for taking the back of an opponent in the turtle position. Taking the back is not as big a subject as passing the guard, but it is a big one, and a book could be written just on it. We won't attempt to survey all those techniques here, but we will offer two basic options.

Here are a few general tips on taking the back:
- Don't put your legs inside of your opponent's.
- Beware of your opponent trapping one of your arms and attempting to roll.
- Keep your hips connected to his.
- Don't be afraid to change your angle, especially if you sense he is setting you up.

White is in the turtle position. Blue holds from the side.

Blue works his hands in under White's armpits and grabs White's wrists.

Blue moves around to White's rear and sits low on White's hips.

White is in the turtle position. Blue holds from the side.

Blue moves around to White's rear and sits low on his hips. Blue grabs inside White's rear collar with both hands.

Blue begins to pull back on White's collar.

Taking the Back

Blue leans back, lifting White up. The insides of his legs control White's hips as he lifts.

Blue puts his hooks in. Note Blue is lifting up under White's arms so he cannot block the hooks.

Blue falls to his side and pulls White over, taking White's back.

Blue pulls White up and pinches White's sides with his knees.

Blue puts both hooks in.

Blue falls back to his side, taking White's back.

Neck crank side control

This technique works because opponents, in an attempt to take away openings you could use to put in your hooks, will make themselves very compact. When they do, they sacrifice some of their base, allowing you to turn them on their side. From their side, they will continue to be concerned with preventing you from hooking your feet in and taking the back. You counter by moving yourself out from under them and pinning their shoulders.

White goes to the turtle position. Controlling from the side, Blue reaches under both of White's armpits and grabs the lapels on both sides. Blue drives his weight into White with his posted right foot.

Blue quickly slides his right knee in close to White's right knee, and simultaneously swings his left knee behind White's rear.

Blue leans back and, using his weight, pulls White onto his right side. As Blue pulls back, he swings his left leg around to his rear for base.

Neck Crank Side Control

> ⊙ This attack is somewhat unorthodox. As a result, White is unprepared for the attack on his neck.

Posting on his left foot, Blue scissors his right leg back and underneath his left.

Blue comes to the sprawl position behind White's head.

Blue moves back away from White and pulls White flat onto his back. Pushing off the balls of his feet, Blue now drives his right shoulder into the back of White's head to force his chin to his chest, resulting in a forward neck crank.

Neck crank side control follow-ups

Once you get to neck crank side control, remember that you have options. You could simply transition to the north/south position or side control. Or, as seen here, you could follow-up with submissions.

Continuing from the north/south sprawl control, Blue reaches around White's neck with his right hand and grabs thumb inside White's left lapel, as high up as possible.

Blue now comes to his knees and turns White onto his right side. Blue releases his left lapel grip and slides his left arm up behind White's neck. Blue chops down with his left hand as he pulls with his right hand to apply the single-wing choke.

Continuing from the previous position, Blue can also set up the armbar. Blue grabs his own lapel with his left hand.

This is another finish from the same position. Blue grips White's left collar with his right hand, thumb in. Blue then reaches straight across with his left hand and grabs White's right lapel, thumb in.

Blue moves to his left and pulls down with his left hand as he pulls back with his right for the sliding collar choke. Blue does not keep his chest tight. To the contrary, he makes space.

Neck Crank Follow-Ups

Blue grabs inside White's right lapel with his right hand and brings his arm in front of White's throat. Blue pushes down with his weight into his right arm to pin Blue to the mat on his side.

Keeping his hips low, Blue swings his right leg over White's head.

Sitting as close as possible to White's shoulder and pinching his knees tight, Blue falls back for the armbar.

◎ **Against an inexperienced opponent, or even as a surprise against an experienced one, put the turtle on his back.**

position

→ **Basic turnover:** Hold your opponent's far side triceps and ankle and drive forward.

→ **Basic turnover:** Drive your chest into his side as you pull his far arm and push off the balls of your feet.

◎ **Attack the arm if your opponent gives your the opening. Your leg is stronger than his arm.**

arm bars

→ **Turtle armlock- straight arm:** Scoop under his near arm with your forward leg. Cross your feet under his wrist and drop your hips into his elbow.

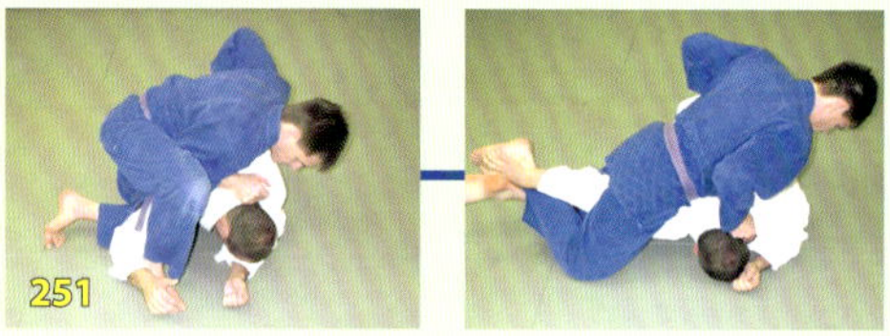

→ **Turtle armlock- arm bent forward:** Switch your hips forward. Your bottom leg comes forward and your top leg pulls his forearm back.

→ **Turtle armlock- arm bent back:** Switch your hips the other way and use your rear leg to torque his elbow Kimura-style.

→ **Kimura roll:** Instead of the previous technique, roll over your inside shoulder to finish his arm Kimura-style.

◎ **Instead of hooking the front leg in front of his arm, push it from behind with your rear leg for the triangle.**

→ **Triangle:** Your rear knee moves under his chest and you scoop under his far arm. Your top leg comes over his head as you sit back and then lock the triangle.

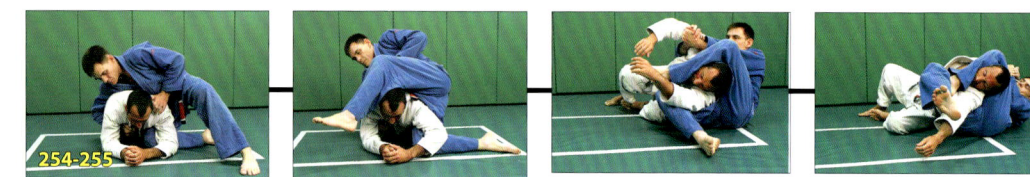

Clock choke: Get a deep collar grip and then drop your hips into your opponent's near shoulder. Use your torso for the power to finish the choke.

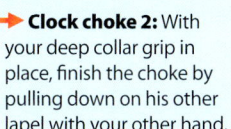  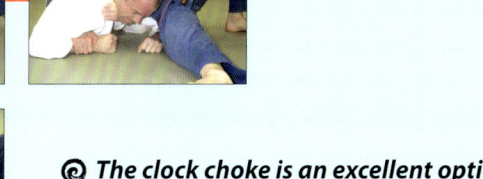

Clock choke 2: With your deep collar grip in place, finish the choke by pulling down on his other lapel with your other hand.

⊙ *The clock choke is an excellent option against the turtle position. If you can set up the lapel grip, you have many options.*

Clock choke 3: Sometimes the key to finishing is to push the back of his head down with your chest.

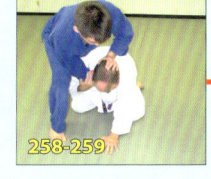 

Clock choke 6: Use the top of your shin to push down his head as your arm pulls up.

Clock choke 4: Push his head down, then step over it with your front leg. The back of your leg pushes down as your arm pulls up.

clock choke series

Clock choke 5: If he tackles your leg as you do #4, hold his belt with your free hand. Straighten out your tackled leg as you pull the collar.

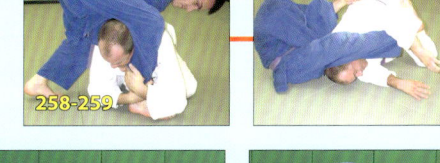

Clock choke 7: Surprise him by lifting your hips and throwing your back leg over and around. You push down on his head with the back of your leg as you pull it with your arm.

▷ **Opposite grip:** If you are gripping the collar on the opposite side as for the clock choke, step over with both legs and then sit back and pull.

▷ **Escape counter:** If he spins into you to take off the choke, switch to an arm bar.

Rolling pass: With a deep collar grip, roll over your rear shoulder. Quickly circle your feet away from him, and bring one leg under the other as you turn belly-down.

▶ **Escape counter:** If he back-rolls out of the rolling pass, maintain your collar grip, and roll with him and back to the clock choke position.

crucifix

Crucifix roll: Scoop up his arm with your forward leg. Hold a collar grip with one hand, and, as you roll forward, scoop under his arm with your other arm.

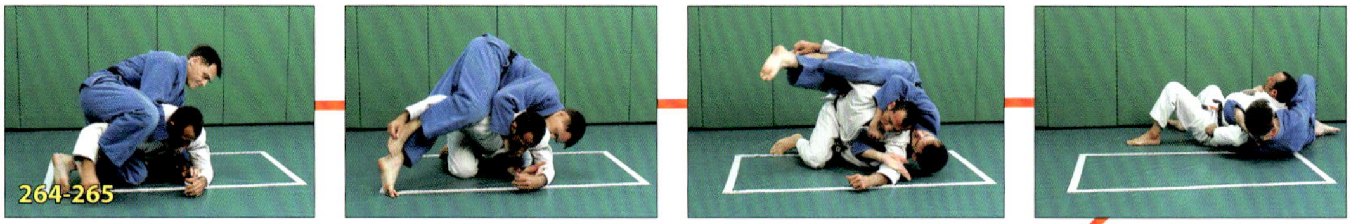

264-265

▲ ...knee behind head

▲ ... leg over

▲ ... single-wing choke

▶ **Crucifix submissions:** Once you roll into the crucifix position, there are many possible submissions....

266-267

▲ ... double-lapel choke

▲ ... arm bar

▲ ... neck crank

belt-grab attacks

Arm bar: From north/south, hold his belt palm-up and drop weight into your elbow. Scoop up his arm, sit on his head, and take the arm.

Arm bar: If you cannot lean back, drop forward.

Surprise key lock: Fake like you are doing the previous move, then spin the opposite way to set up a key lock.

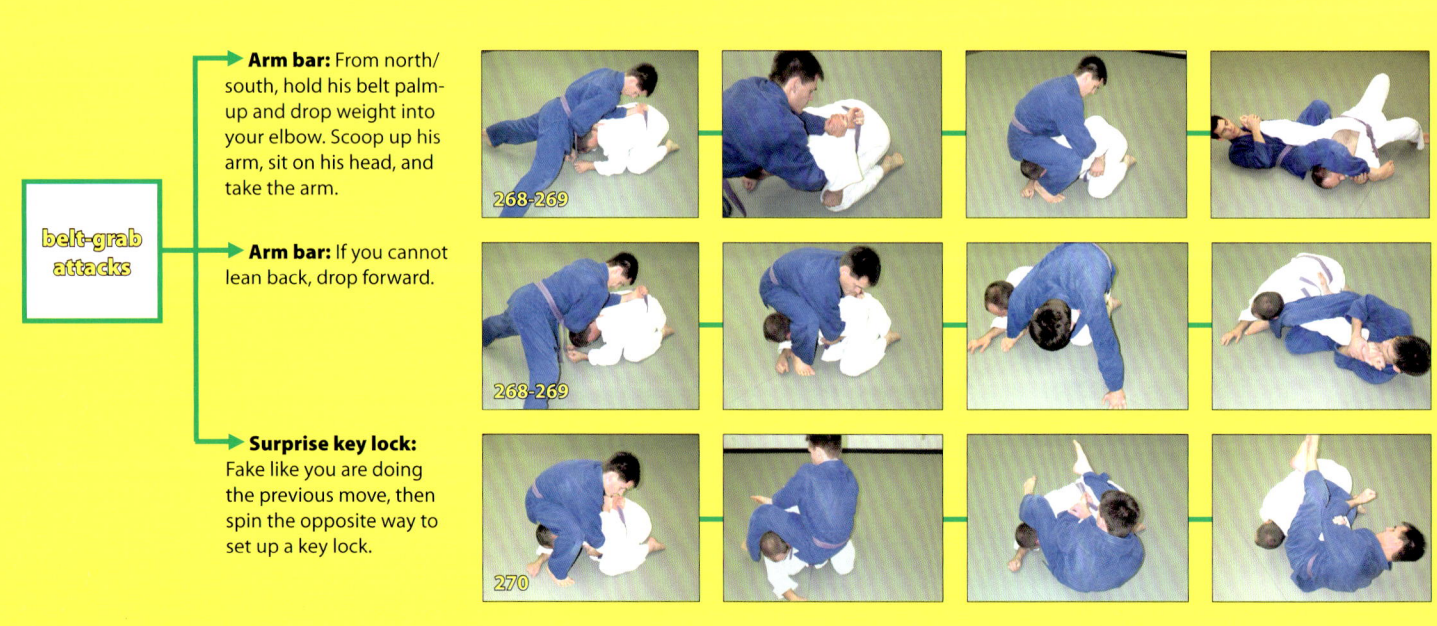

268-269

268-269

270

head and arm chokes and sweeps

Gator roll: Your shoulder comes to his ear, so your arm is in very deep. Make a figure-four and drop your head under. Walk you body so your stomach pushes the back of his head.

271

Collar choke: Get a collar grip, and duck your head under his arm as you roll, like the gator roll. Slide your other arm under the back of his head to lever it up as you turn belly-down.

272-273

Mount: The roll begins as with the last technique. Instead of turning belly-down for the choke, back roll to mount.

274

Mount: Unlike the moves above, here your arm goes under his armpit first, not the head. Roll him over his trapped shoulder, then back-roll to mount.

275

Turnover to choke: Similar to the last technique, go under the armpit to the collar choke. The grip is different, but once again, roll him over his trapped shoulder.

276

Breadcutter: If he makes base against the roll, apply the breadcutter choke.

277

Breadcutter: Instead of going under his armpit first, your bottom arm can simply go straight against his throat.

277

Breadcutter: Here, once again, the bottom arm goes under his armpit first. This sets up the D'Arce if the breadcutter does not make him tap.

277

D'Arce: Drive forward and dive your bottom arm through as far as you can, then apply a figure-four choke.

278-279

guillotine

Arm-in guillotine: Grips and angles are key. Lift him up, and then sit under.

Peruvian necktie: If you cannot lift him, step over him, and use the backs of your legs and your back to increase the pressure.

Guillotine: If you can get the neck by itself, without the arm, this is as basic and effective as it gets.

Ten-finger choke: This guillotine variation relies on trapping the back of his head on your lower abdominals and using that to force his chin down around your hands.

advance the position

Take the back: Start to his side, get double-wrist control. Now when you lift from behind, his hands are not available to block your feet.

Take the back: Yank the back of his collar and then put your hooks in.

To north/south: Get double-under-hook lapel grips, and block his knee with yours. Switch your hips back and forth. Your shoulder pushes his head as you pull his lapels.

Arm bar: Take advantage of your under-hook grips. Attack the arm near your head. Stay tight as you come up, and put your legs over his head and in his armpit.

Choke: Let go with one hand and reach across his throat. Use the under-hook lapel grip of your other hand to feed the lapel to the choking hand.

GrapplingArts.net

Chapter 8

Drills

Solo grappling drills are an important part of training. Practicing solo drills confers two very important benefits. The first is an increase in the physical attributes required for competitive grappling: strength, speed, flexibility, balance, endurance, and agility. These attributes are developed in a task-specific manner, meaning exactly as they will be needed when you are actually grappling. Secondly, drills mimic techniques or aspects of techniques that are actually applied on opponents. Solo practice serves to reinforce correct technique in your muscle memory. The mind has to learn how the body moves; drills are a way of teaching it.

We all know that the best techniques in the world are useless if we are not in good enough shape to apply them. That being said, bear in mind the maxim that you can only cheat yourself when it comes to drills. Drills will help get you in shape while at the same time helping to develop correct movement skills for technique.

The drills in this chapter were selected with passing the guard in mind. Most of the drills shown involve hip and core body movement. Hip movement is key to Brazilian jiu-jitsu (and indeed to many other martial arts and sports). Good hip movement is essential for actualizing a lot of the techniques in this book, especially the trickier ones.

When practicing, look for ways to improve your body movement in terms of efficiency and smoothness. Work out kinks and rough spots. Smoothness requires relaxation and attention to the body's own signals.

At the end of the chapter are two partner drills. Those drills use the partner's weight or position as resistance. Like the solo drills, partner drills serve the dual purpose of conditioning and reinforcing correct movement. Drills, especially partner drills, can be created for virtually any technical movement and are only limited by the practitioner's imagination and ingenuity.

Most techniques can be practiced as drills, and repeating a specific technique over and over is a good drill. When you are practicing a technique for the first time, your partner should not be resisting. Once you get the idea and are executing a new technique with some degree of proficiency, have your partner offer increasing amounts of resistance.

Working on things in isolation, ultimately, is not sufficient. Try playing a game where one player resists 50% or so and the other makes from one to three moves. The players then switch so that the guy who was going half speed gives the other guy a chance to try his moves. Go back and forth. If both guys are not tapping, at least one is resisting too much. The idea is to work on transition, flow, and counters. You both must 'leave your egos at the door' to reap the benefits of this type of training. You do not need to restart every time there is a submission. Instead, back off the submission and let the other guy begin his turn by making some sort of escape.

Even though this type of training is cooperative, it can be quite vigorous. It has the advantage of allowing you to attempt moves in a dynamic situation without significant consequences for failure.

Leg whip-over

This drill is to develop the hip movement necessary for the leg trap passes on pages 80-84. As you bring your leg over, bring it up in a big arch as high as you can.

Lie face down with the arms extended out to the sides. Look to your left.

Whip your left leg back over to your right, putting the sole of your foot on the mat. Try to open the pelvis and point your left knee straight at the ceiling.

Return to the starting position and turn your head to look to the right.

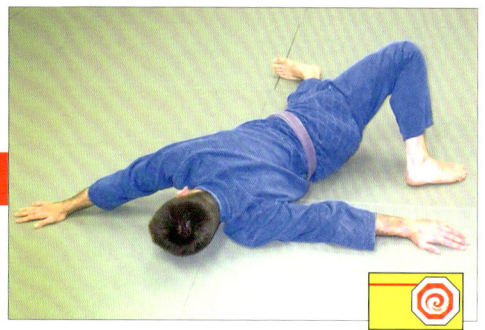

Repeat to the other side. Try to trace a high arching path with your legs.

Diving sprawl

Put your hands down ahead of your body. Kick one foot, then the other, straight up over your head to the handstand position. Slowly bend your arms and lower your chest to the mat. Keep your back arched and roll down the front of your body until your legs are on the mat.

Let the momentum carry your upper body up, and push with your arms into the sprawl position. You should have a spotter catch your feet and help balance you in the handstand position when you are first learning the drill.

Sit-Out Drill #1

The sit-out is a bread and butter wrestling move. In wrestling, it is used primarily as an escape. In jiu-jitsu, it plays an important role in passing the guard and as an escape from the bottom turtle position. On this spread are two variations of sit-out drills. In both instances, note how you post on a hand and the opposite foot. Posting on opposite limbs is a recurring theme in Brazilian jiu-jitsu and a skill that all serious practitioners must have. This first drill should be done side-to-side in a fluid motion. Strive to execute the movement smoothly. Do not touch your butt to the mat.

Start in a squat position with both palms on the ground.

Scissor your right foot across the front of your body to the left. Base on your right hand and left foot.

Extend your right leg as far as possible as you twist your torso to the left, keeping your hip off the mat.

Pull your hips back and begin to retract your leg.

Put your left hand back on the mat, and bend your right leg underneath your body.

Return to the start position.

Sit-out Drill #2

The first part of this movement is the same as in the last drill. This time, however, you will keep rotating in the same direction and post on all fours belly-up. First, you post on your hand and opposite foot on one side, then you switch to posting on your other hand and its opposite foot as you go from belly-up to bell-down, complete the rotation. Examples of the use of this movement include the knee-through-the-middle smash pass follow-ups on pages 32-33 and 116-117.

Start in a sprawl position.

Post on your right hand, and scissor your right leg across to the left.

Post your right foot, and twist your torso to the left, whipping your left hand back over to post on the mat even with your right hand.

Twist up into the face-up all-fours position with your hands and feet parallel.

Continuing, post on your right foot, and thread the left leg back beneath your hips as you twist your body to the left.

Turn over to your left, and reach for the mat with your right hand.

Reach over with your right hand, and post it on the ground in the sprawl position. Now you are where you started, just turned around.

Repeat.

Strive for smoothness and fluidity.

TWIST-AND-FLIP

Like the last two drills, this drill involves posting diagonally. Instead of using a hand and the opposite foot, this time it is a shoulder and the opposite foot. The first four photos depict Blue threading his right leg out from under his left leg; this part of the drill is applicable to the leg trap passes on pgs. 80-84. The second column of photos show Blue flipping over his shoulder and landing on his feet; this applies to the flip-and-turn pass on pages 72-73.

Start on your back with your feet on the mat and your hips raised.

Lift your hips and right foot off the mat.

Thread your right foot behind your left leg.

Posting on your left foot and right shoulder, begin to twist face-down as you move your right arm past your hip toward the rear.

Finish threading your right leg to the rear and post your right foot on the mat. Your feet are parallel and wider than shoulder width. As you post your right foot, begin to tuck your chin toward your chest.

Move your head below your hips.

Initiating the movement with the hips, whip your feet toward the mat.

Land in the bridge position 180° from the start position. You can repeat the exercise on the same side or on the opposite side to return to the start position.

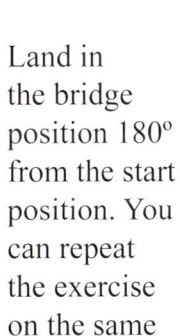

ONE-ARMED PUSH-UPS

We call this a one armed push-up, but the drill is not about using the strength of one arm. To the contrary, you should rely on core body strength. Similar to the last drill, you will thread one leg under the other after posting on one shoulder and the opposite foot. Once you are belly-down and post your arm, most of your weight will then transfer to that arm and the opposite foot. Repeat the drill to both sides while keeping your butt and hips from ever touching the mat.

Lie on your back. Lift your hips and right leg off the mat.

Begin to thread your right leg behind your left.

Post your arm out straight, and then lift your unsupported shoulder using your **torso** to do most of the work.

Now go back the way you came. Posting on your feet and left hand, move your right arm across your chest.

MODIFIED CARTWHEEL

This is a variation on a cartwheel, but starting from a seated position. It is useful for the cartwheel pass from pages 146-147. Even if you do not like that technique, this drill helps with core body control and coordination. Normal cartwheels are also worth practicing for the same reasons.

Sit on your left hip with your right leg bent and your left leg straight. Post your left arm straight behind you. You are in the left sitting guard position.

Pushing off with your right leg, lift you hips and turn to your left. Reach your right arm across your body toward the mat.

Put your right hand down on the mat parallel to your left hand.

Continuing the momentum, swing your straight right leg directly above the head.

One-Armed Push-Ups/Modified Cartwheel

As you thread your right leg to the rear, post up on your right shoulder.

Swing your right arm below your hips to the rear.

Post your right foot parallel to your left, wider than shoulder width. Move your right hand outside your right shoulder in the push-up position.

Posting your right shoulder and left foot on the mat, move your right knee forward under your left leg.

Twist to your left and turn face-up.

Post your right foot next to your left, and return to the original position. Repeat the exercise left and right.

The momentum will carry your left leg up as well. Open your legs, keep your arms straight, and look between your hands.

Lower your right leg straight down to the mat.

Begin twisting to your left and whip your left leg back over your right.

Land in the sitting guard on your right side. Repeat right and left.

Head Spring

Like the twist-and-flip drill on page 298, here you land on your feet. This is a needed skill for the somersault pass on pages 86-87. In the top set of photos, after landing on his feet, Blue uses his arms and bridges. The ability to hold that position is beneficial from a conditioning and flexibility standpoint.

Start kneeling with the top of your head on the mat. Put your palms on the mat on either side of your head.

Straighten your legs and post on your toes. Your torso should be vertical, with the weight distributed between the top of your head and your hands.

Kick both feet over your head and arch your back.

Land on the soles of your feet on the mat, and lift your head. Hold the back-arch position to build strength.

This is the complete drill in motion sequence. After landing on your feet in the back-arch position, lower your head, twist to one side, and roll to your knees.

Hop up & Sprawl

Before you can pass from your feet, you need to be on your feet. The next few drills are for hopping to your feet from your knees in the guard, as in the standing techniques from pages 104-105. The drill on this page also incorporates practicing sprawling. Sprawling is primarily used as a defense against take downs.

Sit in *seiza* with your back straight and your fists on the mat in front of your knees.

Land on the balls of you feet with your legs wide and straight.

Lean your weight into your fists, and lift your hips. Putting your weight into your hips makes your lower body effectively lighter.

Keeping your arms straight and your shoulders back, drop your hips in the full sprawl position.

Keeping your hips as low as possible, pull your feet up into the full squat position as you simultaneously lift your fists off the mat.

Put your palms on the mat.

Contract your abs, and begin to pull your knees toward your chest.

Keep your hips as low as possible as you pull up your feet.

Lean your weight into your hands, and throw your feet back.

Come back to the sprawl, and repeat, or drop back to the *seiza* position, and repeat.

JUMPING UP FROM THE KNEES

This is a drill that builds explosive strength from sitting on the feet. This movement is useful when jumping to the standing position from the guard. It also builds coordination between the upper and lower body.

Sit on your heels. Begin by swinging your arms over your head to help lift the weight of your upper body off your legs. As you hips begin to rise, contract your abs and pull your knees up toward your chest. Pull your feet up under your hips, and land in the full squat position.

> ◉ Variation: You can make the exercise more challenging by rotating your body 90 degrees in the air as you spring up.

Partner Lift

This partner drill incorporates elements of the last two techniques. This time, however, once you get to your feet, you lift your partner up by his lapels. Obviously, you are going to need to exert yourself, which is the point. Try for twenty repetitions. This is a conditioning drill, but the ability to pick up your opponent is a valuable skill. Sometimes it is the best way to deal with a difficult closed guard. Make sure not to slam your opponent on the way down, because this is a drill, and because it is harder not to.

Sit in your partner's closed guard. Grab both lapels high up on your partner's collar.

Stand up.

Keeping your back straight, squat a little and arch back, lifting your partner off the mat. Try to pull your partner's forehead up towards your own.

Lower your partner to the mat slowly.

Drop back to the kneeling position.

> As you stand, post with your arms and shift your weight forward. Doing so will make popping up easier.

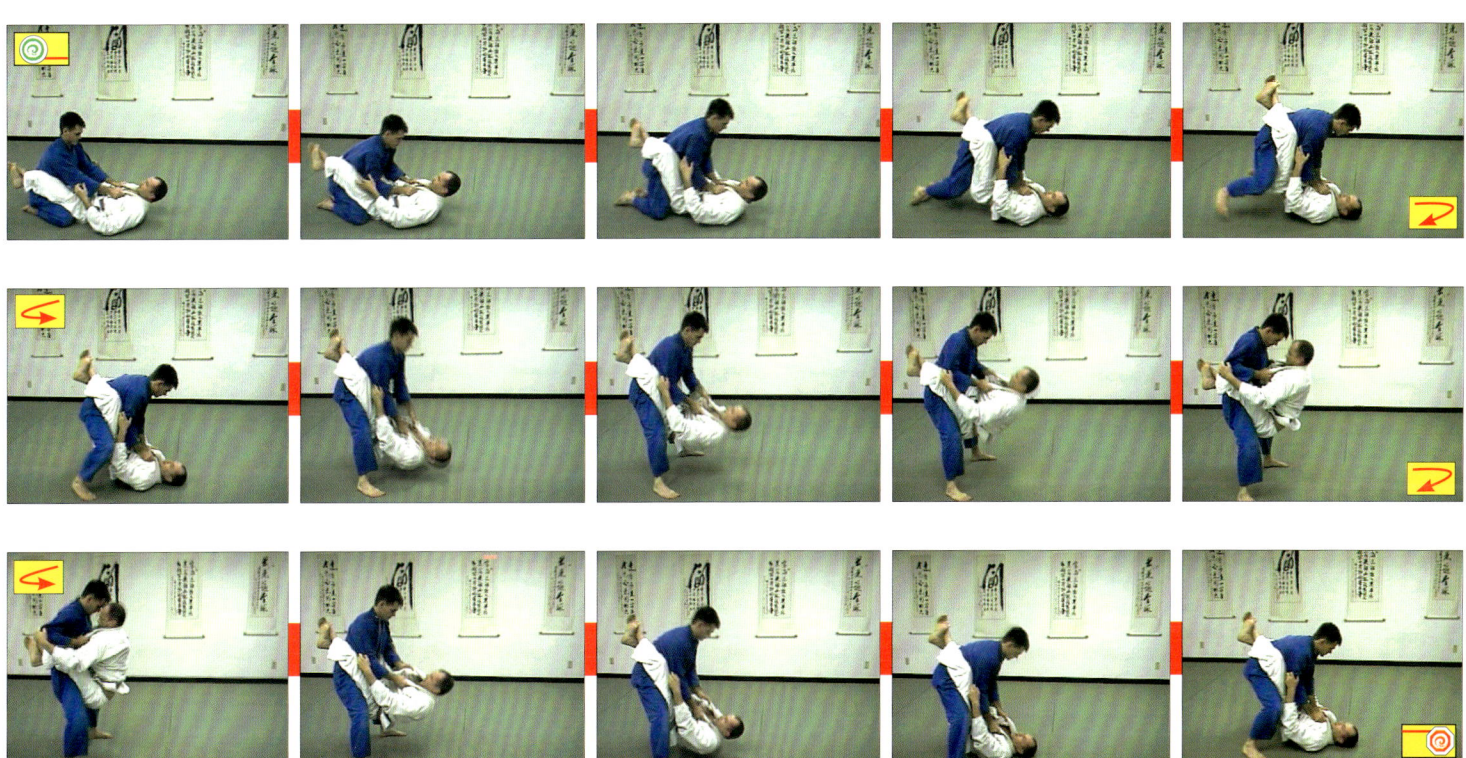

Knee-on-belly drill

This drill emulates the bull-fighter guard pass. You can turn just about any technique into a drill by repeating it from side to side. Create your own drill with that in mind. Remember that jiu-jitsu evolves because of innovations. Innovations come from experimentation in dojo laboratories around the world. Those innovations can come from anyone, yourself included.

Your partner lies on his back with his knees bent. Bend forward, and grab inside your partner's knees, thumbs back.

Push your partner's knees to your right, and simultaneously cross-step your right foot to the outside of your partner's right hip.

Step up with your left foot and post the foot outside your partner's head as you drop your right knee to the knee-on-belly position.

Step your left leg back to its starting position.

Step your right leg back around to its starting position.

Repeat the drill to the opposite side.

The exercise should be repeated smoothly to the left and right. Concentrate on precision and getting to a solid knee-on-belly stance with most of your weight on your opponent's belly and your other leg straight, sole of the foot on the mat.

◎ Try to do the move smoothly. For that matter, try to do all your drills and techniques smoothly. Constantly iron out the kinks in your movements. There is always some detail you can improve on. Learn to recognize those details.

Matte!

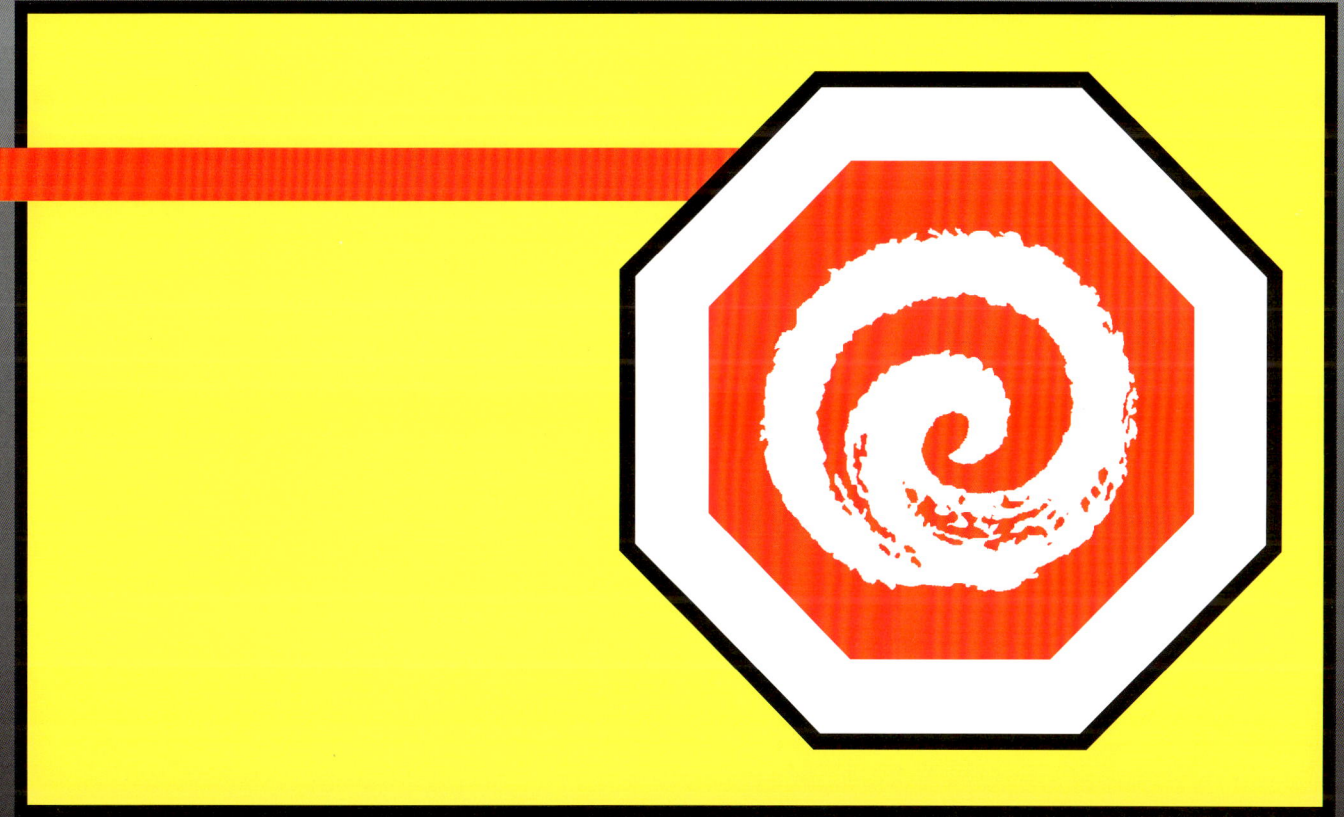

Complete the trilogy!

The Guard

The Guard covers the fundamentals of body movement from the bottom position. The volume is loaded with attacking techniques and features Joe Moreira's favorite strategies and sequences from the guard. Includes chapters covering chokes, armbars versus a stacking opponent, attacking defensive/stalling posture, neck control attacks, the turtle position, and much more. The revised second edition includes thumbnail flowchart summaries, an additional chapter not found in the original, and crisper, cleaner image quality.

Strategic Guard

The companion to *The Guard* is the first and only book to examine in detail how to obtain, maintain, and retain the guard position. Over 2800 photos in 262 pages. Includes thumbnail flowchart summaries, just like *The Guard*, and cross-referencing to *The Guard*. Detailed coverage of guard-pass counters and submission defense for the guard player. Also includes offense, with chapters on sitting guard and strategies on using the under-hook from the sitting guard.

Visit us at:
GrapplingArts.net

free downloads:
  extra chapters
  excerpts
  bonus material
  favorite techniques
  articles